TUTU

BOB CAREY

We dedicate this book to every person who has been touched by this
life-changing illness.

©2019 Bob Carey

All rights reserved. No part of this book may be reproduced or transmitted in
any form or by any means, electronic or mechanical, without written permission
from the publisher.

Library of Congress Cataloging-in-Publication Data Available

ISBN: 978-0-9858583-4-6

Photographer: Bob Carey
Design: ps:studios, Phoenix, AZ

thetutuproject.com
bobcarey.com

Love, Light and Laughter: The Tutu Project

by Kathleen Vanesian

What started sixteen years ago as a silly, off-the-cuff photo taken by artist photographer Bob Carey has mushroomed into what has now become the world renowned Tutu Project. It all began when burly, bare-chested Carey photographed himself in little more than white socks and a pink tulle tutu left over from a Ballet Arizona photo shoot he did *pro bono* in Phoenix, Arizona. That first image was serendipitously captured in 2003 during a visit with a photographer friend in Santa Fe as the couple was relocating their commercial photographic business from Arizona to New York City. Later that same year, Carey's wife, Linda Lancaster Carey, was diagnosed with an aggressive form of breast cancer, for which she is still undergoing therapy to this day.

Little did the couple know that Bob's repeated photographic attempts to make Linda laugh while she underwent punishing radiation and chemotherapy treatments would eventually blossom into a nonprofit enterprise solely dedicated to raising funds for organizations devoted to nitty gritty financial and emotional support for breast cancer patients and survivors. "Dare2Tutu," The Tutu Project's annual 2-month long fundraising campaign, was kicked off in 2015 and has attracted major corporate sponsors, small businesses, community groups and individuals across the country (for complete details and the opportunity to personally participate in this ongoing project, go to thetutuproject.com). Funds are also raised from the sale of Carey's expertly executed fine art prints featuring his Man in The Tutu.

It is the mundane, everyday needs of breast cancer patients to which the Careys have continually addressed their fundraising efforts: transportation or gas money to get to essential medical treatments, food in the fridge, the payment of unrelenting utility bills or an overdue mortgage payment to ward off the threat of foreclosure. The Tutu Project has donated special chemo shirts to a Maryland hospital stylishly designed to help women feel powerful and beautiful while battling breast cancer. The project provides "cheer packages" to breast cancer patients that include, among other items, a pink tutu, which many patients have actually worn to treatment appointments. "It's funny how a tutu brings such joy and adds a touch of silliness — a welcome break from the devastating reality of a breast cancer diagnosis," explains Linda Carey, who is all too familiar with the problems associated with dealing with this disease.

In The Tutu Project's first fundraising book of photographs, *Ballerina*, Bob Carey's pink tutu popped up in a variety of unlikely urban and rural settings, including, but not limited to, the middle of New York City's Times Square, a beach in sight of San Francisco's Golden Gate Bridge, a deserted dirt road in Utah's Monument Valley, a seaside roller coaster in New Jersey and the solemn grandeur of Washington DC's Lincoln Memorial. In this new compilation, Carey continues to explore themes of isolation, vulnerability and anxiety in the face of danger in far-flung locations worldwide, as well as pastoral and urban settings here in the US.

Carey's instantly recognizable character is reminiscent of Charlie Chaplin's Little Tramp, the star of America's early silent film era. There is a mythic quality to the artist's barefoot Man in The Tutu braving unexplored territory, armed with nothing more than curiosity, trepidation and, ultimately, hope. A classic visual metaphor for man butting heads with the seemingly insurmountable, his implausibly heroic character simultaneously invokes the comic and the poignant — a cross between the slyly mischievous and a mix of dread, awe and joyous optimism. As Chaplin used his Little Tramp persona — decked out in bowler hat, baggy trousers, floppy over sized shoes, a whip-like walking cane and toothbrush mustache — to examine social issues of his day caused by burgeoning industrialism, Carey subliminally harnesses his Man in The Tutu to effect social consciousness about the destructive effects of breast cancer. Its tentacles grip not only its randomly chosen victims, but also the family, friends and communities of those struck by the disease.

His efforts have not gone unrewarded. In fact, Carey's Man in The Tutu photographs, like much enduring art, comforts, inspires and provokes viewers to creativity and, ultimately, activism. Children especially realize the power of Carey's unspoken permission to limitlessly dream and imagine, as evidenced by *Where is Bob?*, a priceless book of drawings by first graders at Phoenix's Kyrene Traditional Academy created around Tutu stickers given to them by The Tutu Project.

If laughter is truly the best medicine, you, the reader, have in your hand a powerful, no-prescription-required antidote to a very real epidemic.

ROCKS CENTRAL PARK, NEW YORK, NEW YORK 2015

Monument Valley

When I was 15 years old, a friend who inspired me to become a photographer and I drove to Monument Valley in Utah; it's a very spiritual place for me, though it's changed a lot since my first visit (now, there's a hotel right on the rim looking down into the valley). Recently, my friend Doc and I spent the night at this hotel. Nearby, there's an overlook with a very well-known sandstone rock, once windblown and beautifully textured, that Ansel Adams photographed back in the late 50s. Today, that same rock is completely worn from countless people walking and standing on it over the years. It's been pretty much destroyed.

We got up at sunrise to set up our shot at the location that's one of the most photographed views on the planet. I set my camera up early, before anyone else. Unfortunately, the area quickly filled with tourists with the same idea. It wasn't long before there were 50 to 60 tourists shooting the same sunrise.

In the shot it looks like I'm the only one there, but if I would have panned my camera a little to the right, you would have seen hoards of tourists all jockeying to get their shots. When I finished, three families from Japan recognized me and wanted to get their picture taken with The Man in The Tutu. I was gratified that they still remembered our project.

MITTENS MONUMENT VALLEY, UTAH 2016

FRANCO ISLAND BEACH STATE PARK, NEW JERSEY 2019

FORT HANCOCK SANDY HOOK, NEW JERSEY 2015

Supreme Court

My cousin asked me to take a photograph in front of the US Supreme Court building the next time I was in Washington DC. Her husband is a United States District Judge for the US District Court for the District of Arizona and she wanted to surprise him for his birthday with a print. On one of my Washington trips to meet with one of the foundations The Tutu Project supports, I decided to get the shot. We went to the US Supreme Court, set up a tripod, and I wiggled into my tutu. A building guard approached us and asked if what I was doing was for commercial purposes. I said no and explained why I was there. She checked with her boss, who said that it was fine as long as it wasn't for commercial purposes. We were ten minutes into the shoot when a new security guard walks up to me. He looked at me. I looked at him. I asked if he wanted to know what we were doing. He just looked at me and said, "I think I know all I need to know." Then he turned around and walked away.

UNITED STATES SUPREME COURT WASHINGTON D.C. 2019

SUNSET PANCAKE BAY ONTARIO, CANADA 2018

Swan

About a half-mile from where I live, there's a lovely little lake that's home to two swans. It's one of my favorite places to visit in the wintertime, with its untouched snow, stark landscape and muted color palette. I thought it might be funny to make an image that looked like I was communicating with the swans. I put my tutu on and headed for the lake.

When I started taking pictures, the swans swam directly up to me. In the meantime, somebody had called the police to report this half-naked man out on the lake dam in a pink tutu. Police officers arrived and approached me in a pretty unfriendly manner, ordering me to put my clothes on immediately, since all I had on was ladies' pink athletic shorts under my tutu and no shoes.

This apparently was beyond the pale for my sleepy little town. I put my pants and shirt on, then politely asked the police to have their dispatcher check The Tutu Project online, which would explain everything. Within a minute, one of the officers came back to me and asked, "How's your wife doing?" The situation was diffused. Their whole perception of me changed once they looked at the website. With all the crazy stuff going on in the world today, it's no wonder everyone is on high alert. I should add that the officers now donate to The Tutu Project.

SWAN SADDLE RIVER, NEW JERSEY 2014

Zebra

Yes, that's a real zebra in this shot and, no, I was not at a zoo when I photographed him. This was taken at Dun Hollow Stables, the foremost equine boarding and training facility in New Jersey, home to over 75 horses on its sprawling, 31-acre property. Dun Hollow is one of our most recent fundraising sponsors; when we visited them, all the stable staff were dressed in tutus for our arrival.

We scoped out the stables and grazing pastures for potential shots and stumbled onto an old wooden arena that had really beautiful lighting coming in from top and sides — perfect for a good tutu backdrop. The stable owner, Eugene, approached me and asked if I wanted to photograph his zebra. I don't know what I expected to see, but he led me to a stall with a certified-genuine, one-year-old zebra with gorgeous stripes. I set up my camera and the owner brought him out to be photographed.

The zebra was pretty skittish (apparently, they're hard to train) and really not having it. I tried to hold his reins, but he took off, though he did come back eventually. Zebras sound more like donkeys than horses, and seem to run differently than horses, which surprised me. I tried to hold his reins again while putting my arm around his neck, but he ran off again. Finally, he let me get the shot. Sometimes, you stumble onto strange and wonderful things when you least expect it.

ZEBRA DUN HOLLOW STABLES, ALLENTOWN, NEW JERSEY 2019

STATUE OF LIBERTY LIBERTY STATE PARK JERSEY CITY, NEW JERSEY 2013

WATER TANK PARK RIDGE, NEW JERSEY 2013

PELL STREET NEW YORK, NEW YORK 2013

1 AM TIME SQUARE, NEW YORK, NY 2019

LOW TIDE PROVINCETOWN, MASSACHUSETTS 2017

Bloomingdale's Chevy Chase

Our longtime sponsor, Bloomingdale's, has always pretty much let me do whatever I want when I make my pictures. On this particular occasion, we were at the Bloomingdale's in Chevy Chase, Maryland. My standard M.O. is to scout the location to see where the best photo might be and often ask permission to do something, even though I suspect there's no way they're going to let me do it. We went out to see the store front and I see this little shelf above the entrance. I set my camera up and then asked store staff, "Do you have a ladder? I want to climb up on that ledge."

I see Linda slowly shaking her head — but she's used to my hair brained stunts. Bloomingdale's very accommodating staff said, "No problem. We'll get you a ladder." So I climb up in my tutu, carefully walk across the ledge to the right spot and sit down with my legs dangling over the edge. Nobody thought about liability or lawsuits — it was just a communal effort to make sure we got the best picture possible. I'm sure we would have given the store's corporate risk management team a heart attack had they seen what we were doing.

BLOOMINGDALE'S CHEVY CHASE, MARYLAND 2014

TWO LIGHTS ATLANTIC CITY, NEW JERSEY 2016

ZABRISKIE POINT DEATH VALLEY, CALIFORNIA 2017

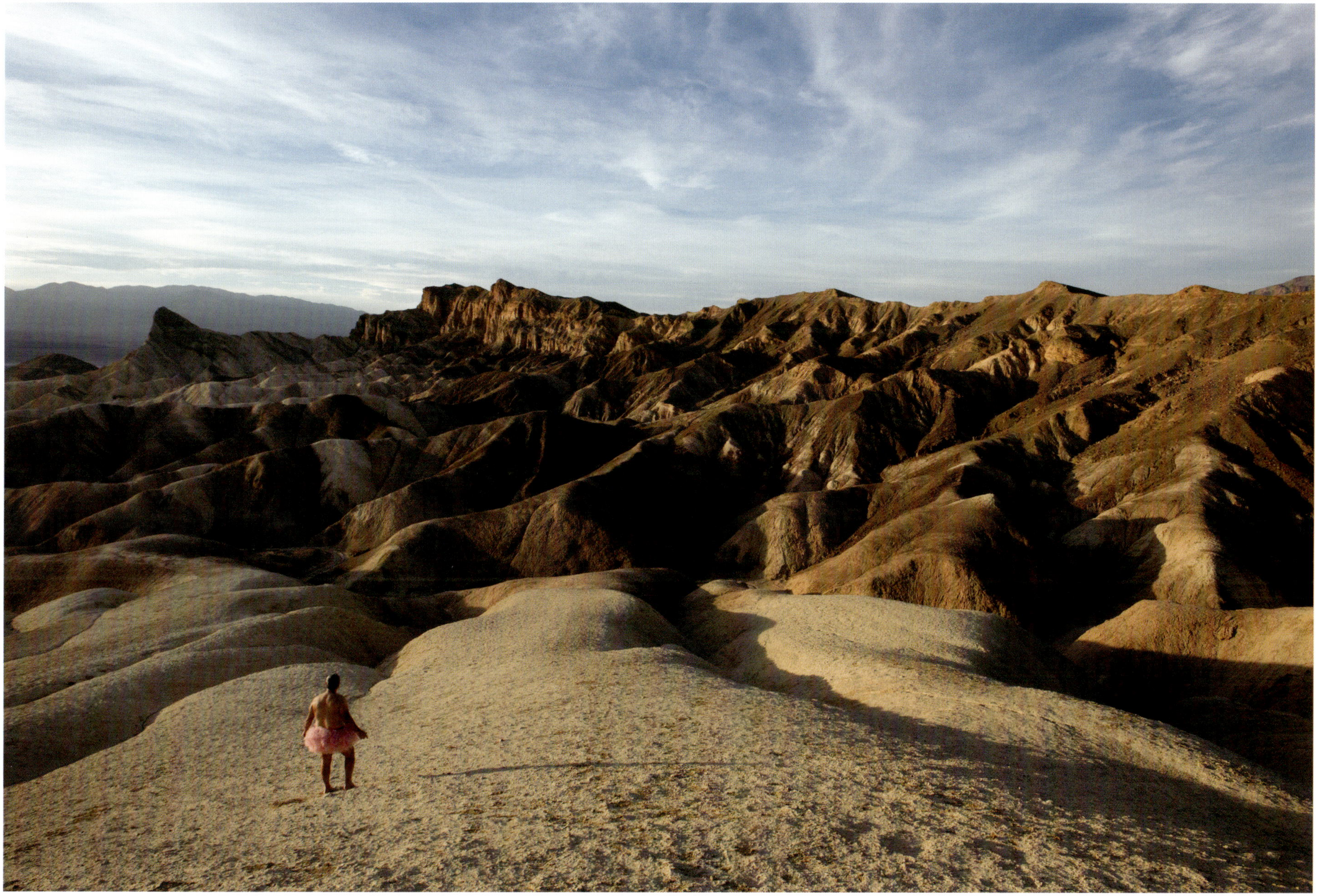

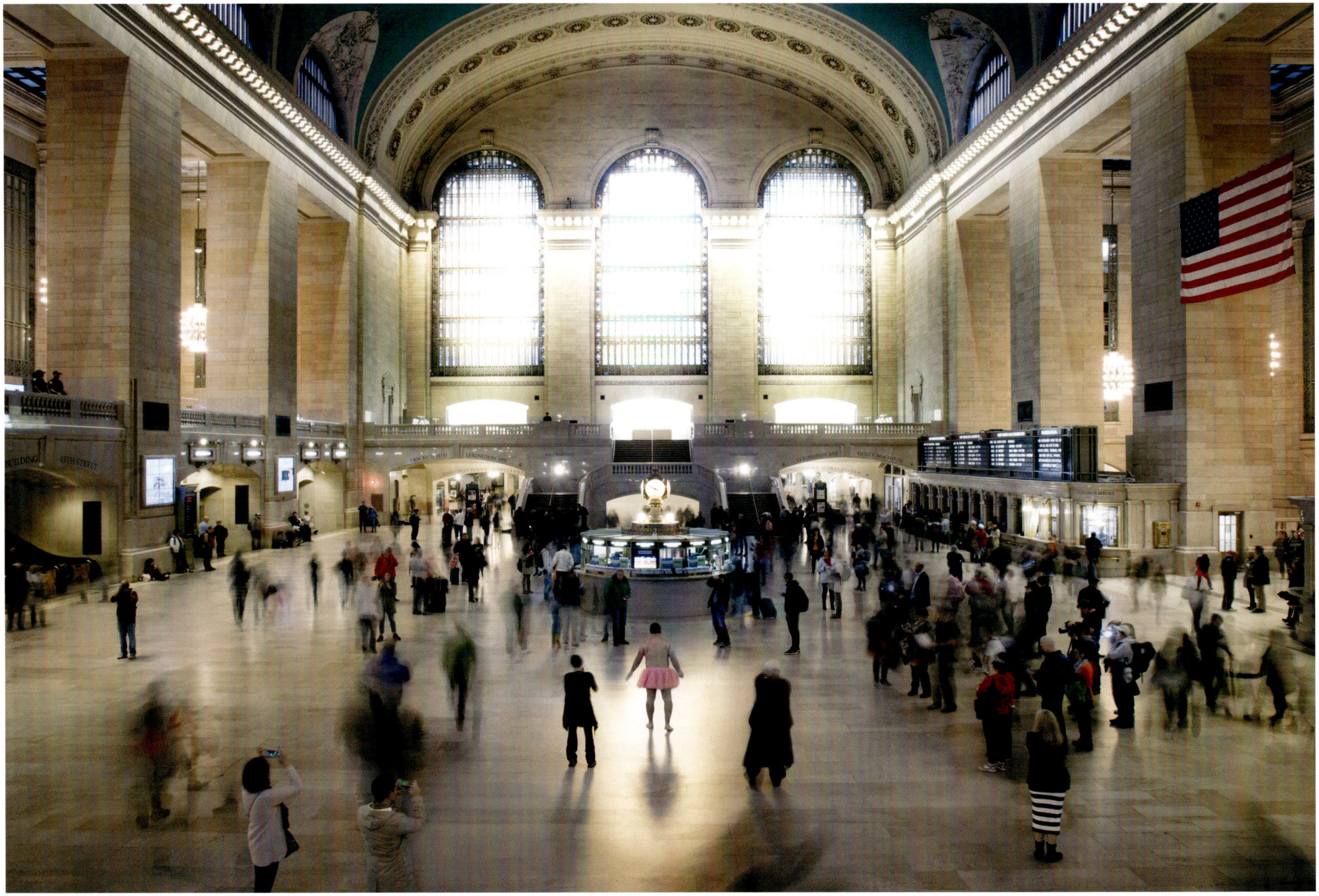

Grand Central Station

When we launched our first Dare2Tutu campaign, we were photographing in the NY area with our fans. As we were shooting in the middle of Times Square, it began to pour, so we moved into Grand Central Station. Since the train station is such a public place, I didn't bother asking for permission to photograph there. I just plopped my tripod down and started shooting with a slow shutter speed, so that some parts of the images would blur. People were taking pictures of me as I was working, which made for a downright surreal atmosphere.

At one point, I looked back at my tripod, which was up high on a staircase, and saw two police officers armed with assault rifles flanking the camera. Uh oh. I just knew I was in big trouble. I walked up to my wife, Linda, and Marcela, our manager, who were securing the camera, as they were talking to the officers. I heaved a sign of relief when I found out that one of the officers was a photographer and loved our project. He was just happy to meet us and offered to give us access to various secret locations in the building.

GRAND CENTRAL STATION MAIN CONCOURSE NEW YORK, NEW YORK 2015

AZ Cardinals

Throughout the entire Tutu Project, unbelievable opportunities have come our way, one of which was through the NFL. The Arizona Cardinals asked us to shoot an image during one of their games and we jumped at this once-in-a-lifetime chance.

They gave me 45 seconds to take a photograph during a commercial break. We had the camera perfectly positioned and manned by my assistants. The idea was that I was going to run out in front of the 70,000 people in the stands and take the photograph. I was held back by a producer of CBS until the right moment. But, while we had permission from the Cardinals, someone forgot to tell the Sheriff's Department that I was going to do this.

After we got the shot, I went back to the room where the producers were gathered. One of the sheriff's deputies approached me and said, "I was running out after you to tase you when, luckily, Cardinal security called me off. We didn't know that this was happening, so we were going to 'take care of you'." I thought to myself, "I wish you would have done it; it would have been awesome. I would have literally taken one for the team."

ARIZONA CARDINALS CHEERLEADERS GLENDALE, ARIZONA 2012

41

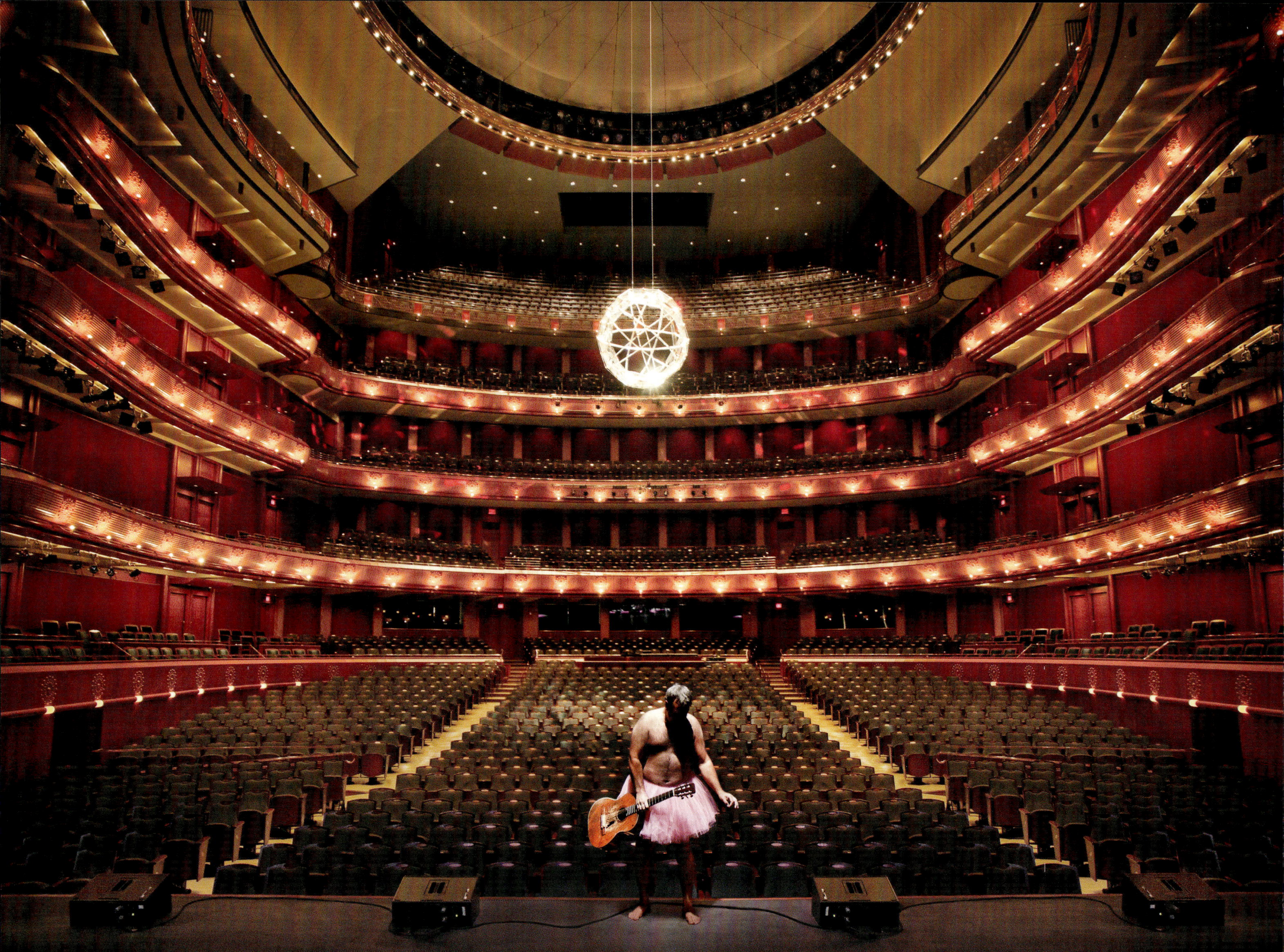

Trigger

For almost 20 years, I've been good friends with the harmonica player for country music legend Willie Nelson. Whenever he's in town, we hang out together and I've gotten to know other band members, the crew, and even met Willie once. My friend thought it would be great if I got up on stage during a show to create a tutu picture. Unfortunately, the opportunity never really presented itself.

One day I was at one of Willie's venues in New Jersey and my friend suggested I use Willie's guitar in my set up. I was in this beautiful auditorium filled with empty seats. Since my shots are often about isolation and loneliness, I decided to shoot toward the empty seats. I asked if I could hold Trigger, Willie's guitar, one of the most famous guitars in the entire world. As I'm standing there grasping the guitar with one hand, all I remember was being repeatedly warned, "Whatever you do, *do not drop the guitar!*"

TRIGGER NJPAC, NEWARK, NEW JERSEY 2012

Shangri-La Hotel, Taipei, Taiwan

Linda and I were invited to shoot a tutu image in Taipei, Taiwan for Marie Claire Magazine; Marie Claire had written about The Tutu Project five years ago, which inspired the magazine to sponsor a fundraising Tutu Run every year since the article appeared. We felt it was a tremendous honor.

Right before we were supposed to leave, Linda got really sick with bronchitis and a nasty sinus infection, which prevented her from flying with me to Taipei. I was put up by the magazine at Shangri-La's Far Eastern Plaza Hotel, a super-luxurious hotel overlooking the spectacular Taipei 101, formerly known as the Taipei World Financial Center. At 101 floors, Taipei 101 was the largest building in the world until the 2010 completion of the Burj Kalifa in Dubai, United Arab Emirates. No matter – it's still outrageously beautiful by any standards.

The Shangri-La treated me like royalty and graciously gave me permission to shoot the 101 from the hotel's rooftop pool area. I literally had only one shot at the image of me diving into the hotel pool, which I never imagined I could pull off, especially 43 stories in the air. The on-site Marie Claire and hotel staff were incredibly helpful in making this work.

When I did the dive, I lost my glasses, which had sunk to the pool bottom. The pool attendant cheerfully retrieved them with a nearby leaf scooper, joking that we were pulling in a big fish. Everyone from the hotel and magazine could not have been nicer or more accommodating. The whole experience is still like a surreal dream to me. I just wish Linda could have been there with me.

ROOFTOP DIVE SHANGRI-LA HOTEL, TAIPEI, TAIWAN 2019

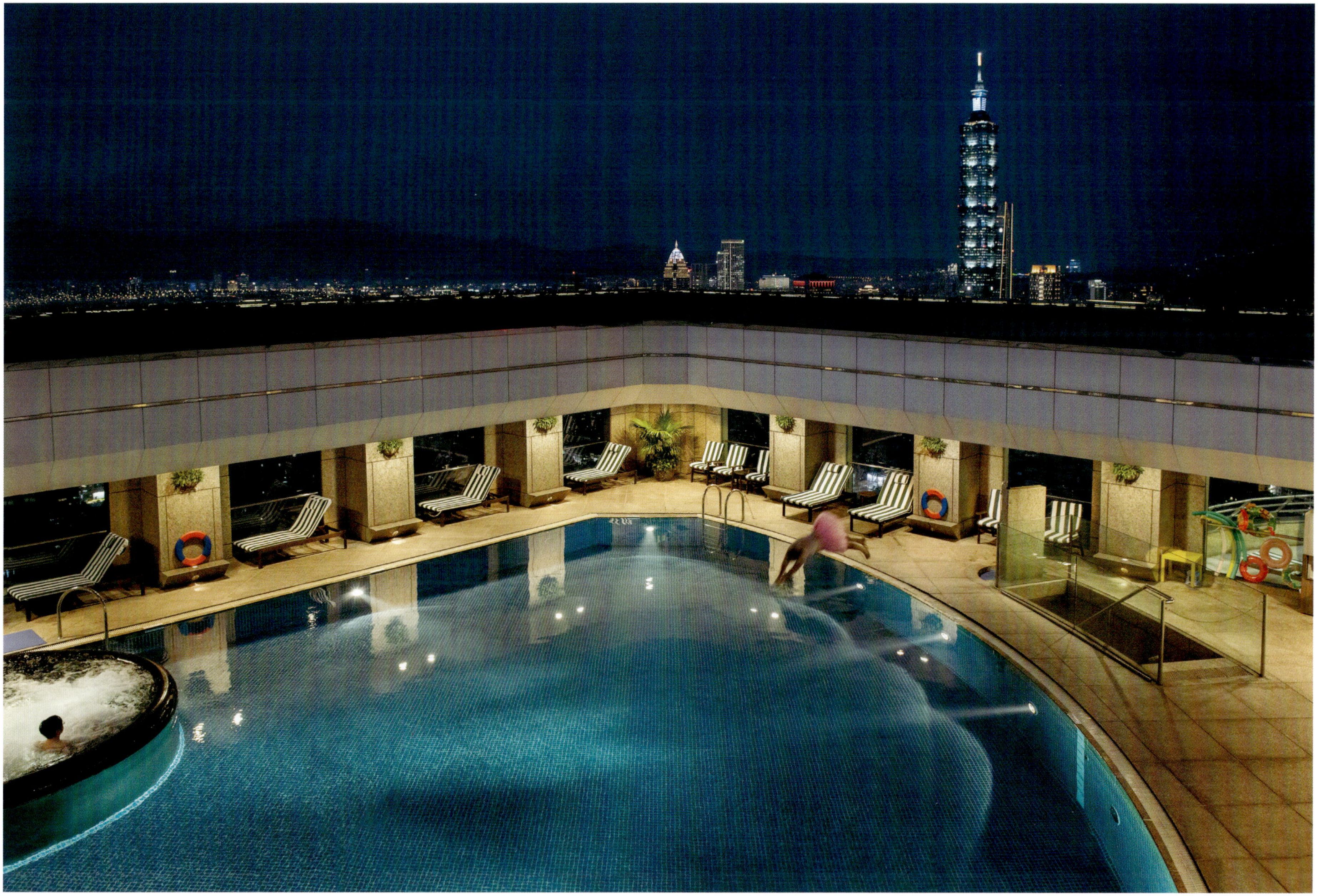

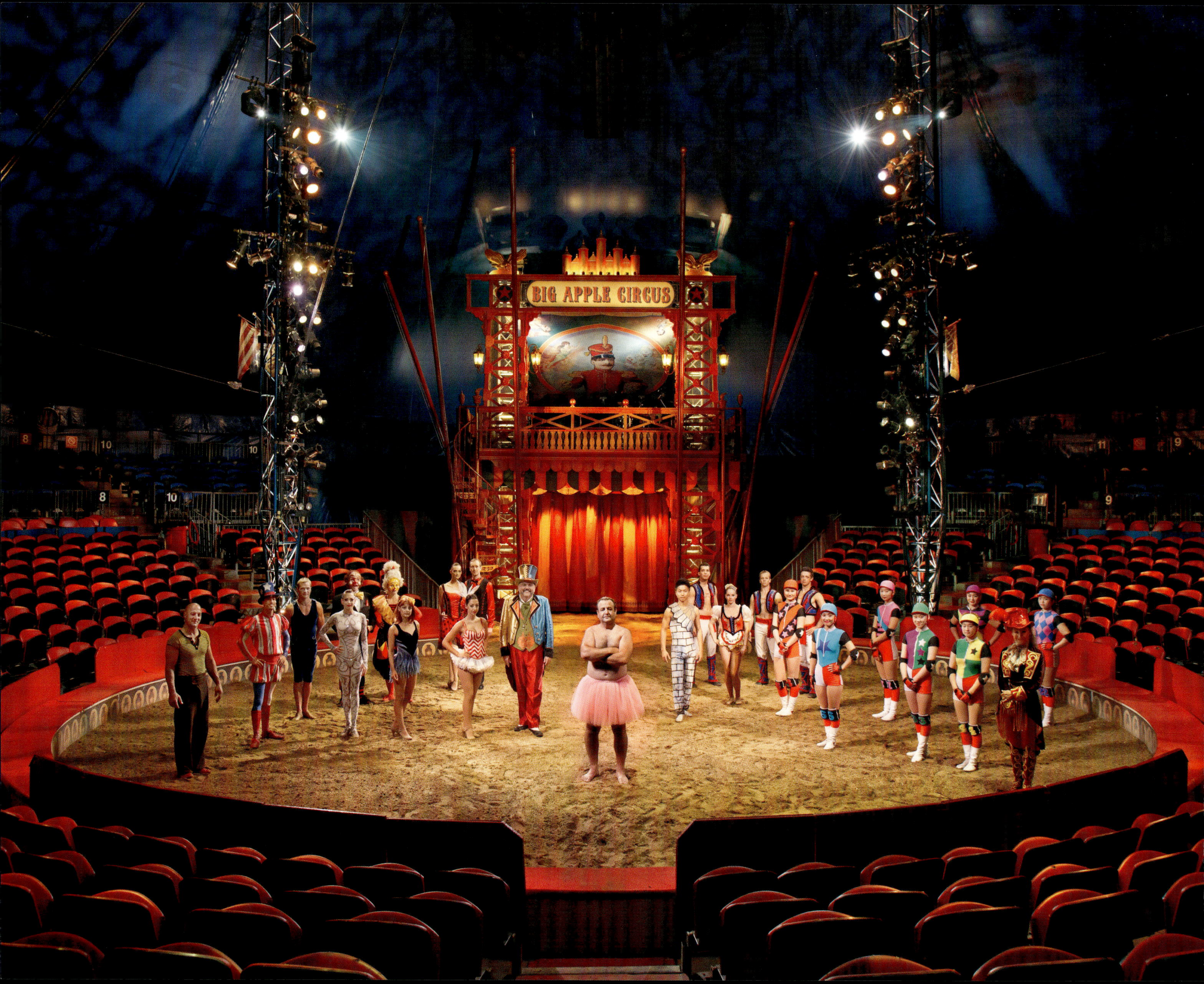
BIG APPLE CIRCUS

BIG APPLE CIRCUS LAKE GEORGE, NEW YORK 2013

PIER AT LONG BEACH ISLAND NEW JERSEY 2015

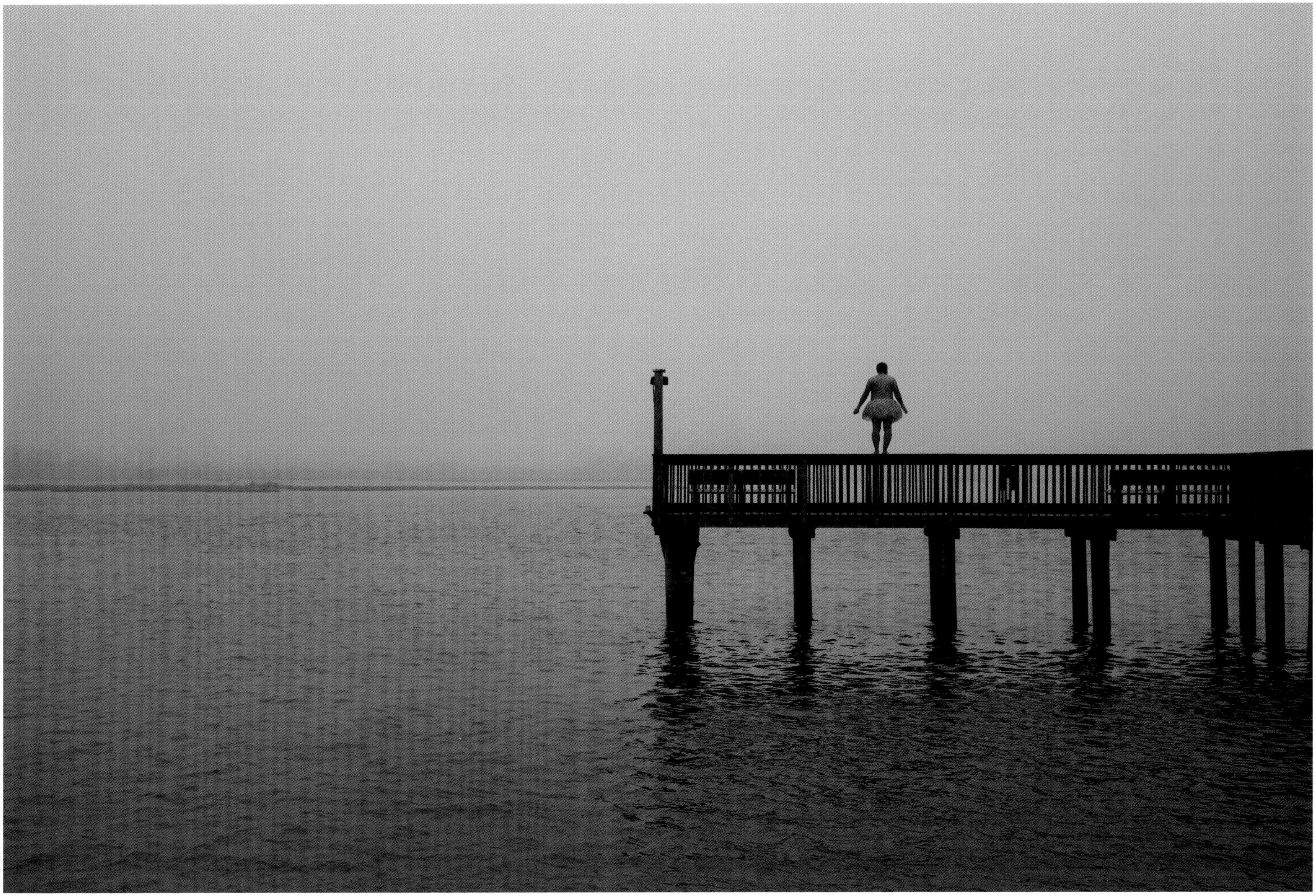

50

Four Dogs

I love when it snows in New York City, especially in Central Park, where the trees are stripped bare by winter. This particular morning, we drove to Central Park after it snowed and went straight to the park's mall, a very iconic location. We began shooting a somewhat normal shot on a beautiful morning, snow slowly melting on the asphalt. Then I spot these four elegant dogs being walked by their owner. I ran over to Marcela, who was assisting me, and asked if she would talk to the guy to see whether I could use his dogs in a photograph. He was very happy to lend me his dogs. They all behaved beautifully and we got the shot. And, of course, only in New York would the owner ask if he needed to sign a model release for the dogs.

FOUR DOGS CENTRAL PARK NEW YORK, NEW YORK 2017

STUDIO 7, BOSTON BALLET BOSTON, MASSACHUSETTS 2017

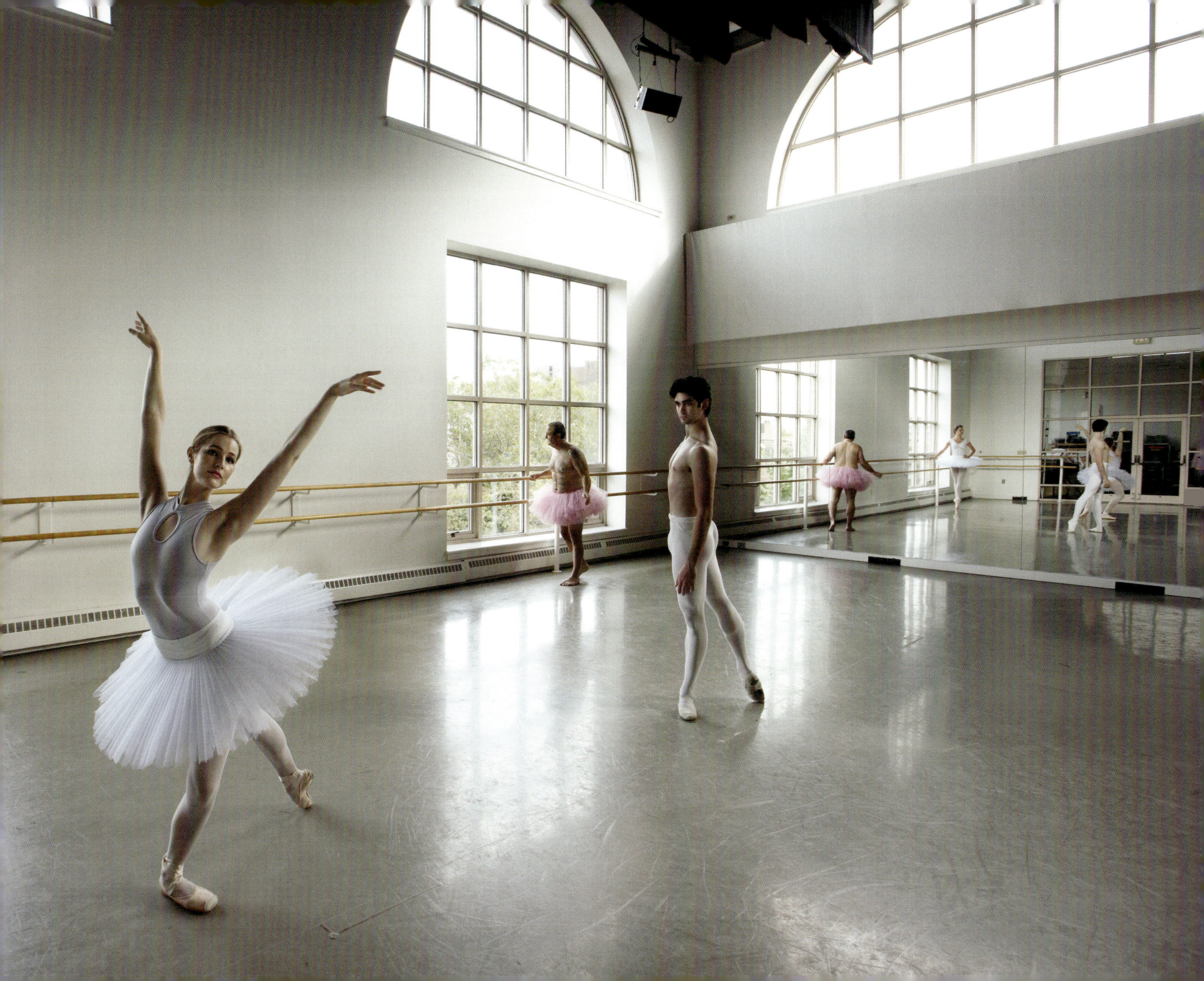

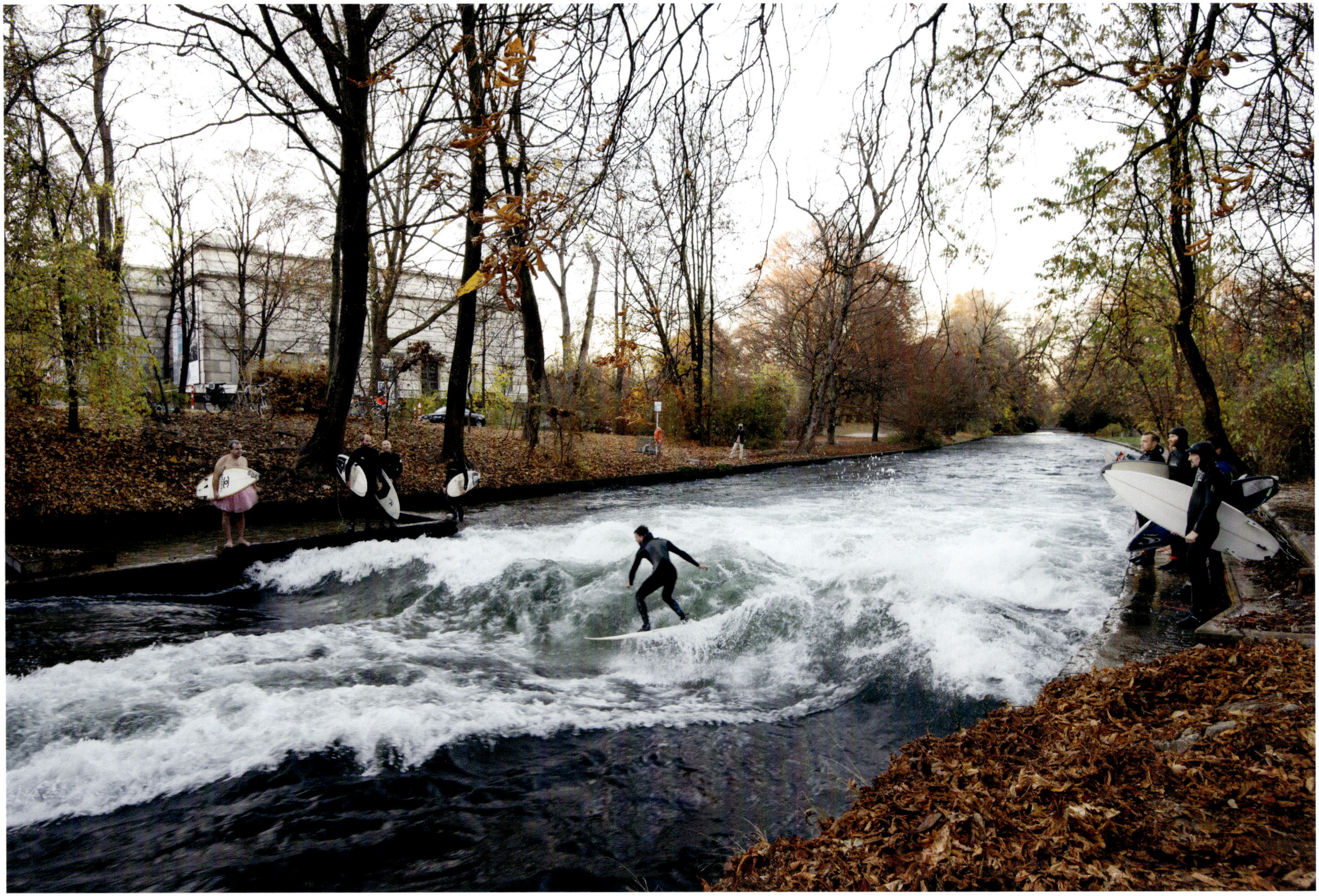

EISBACH WAVE MUNICH, GERMANY 2015

ATM Dickson TN

Several months before we got this shot, Linda's brother, Danny, unexpectedly died of a heart attack in Tennessee. We drove with my sister-in-law, Patti, 15 hours straight through to the memorial that was held for him in a small town outside of Nashville; almost immediately, we turned around and drove 15 hours back home, but not before capturing this image.

Several years before, when Danny and his wife, Ellen, had visited us, they told us about a freestanding brick ATM built on the side of a rural farm road – basically in the middle of nowhere – by a Farmer Clark and his brother, who had bought this 6,000 pound structure and relocated it there.

The day of the memorial was understandably sad. With heavy hearts, we all talked about Danny after the memorial open house. I really wanted to do a tutu shot with the ATM Danny had told us about, so we told the family what we planned to do. Struck by the idea and never having seen us shoot, a group of family members said they were going with us. During the twilight shoot, Linda noted that, instead of being sad, the 3 carloads of family who came to watch were unexpectedly excited at being there to witness me peel off my shorts and climb into my tutu. Linda later said it was like a big, warm hug at the end of a very sad day.

While we were shooting, Farmer Clark came off his field and approached us. We thought for sure he was going to kick us off his property, but it turns out he was excited about us being there and told us the story behind the ATM. I don't think he even noticed I was dressed in a pink tutu.

ATM HOUSTON COUNTY, TENNESEE 2019

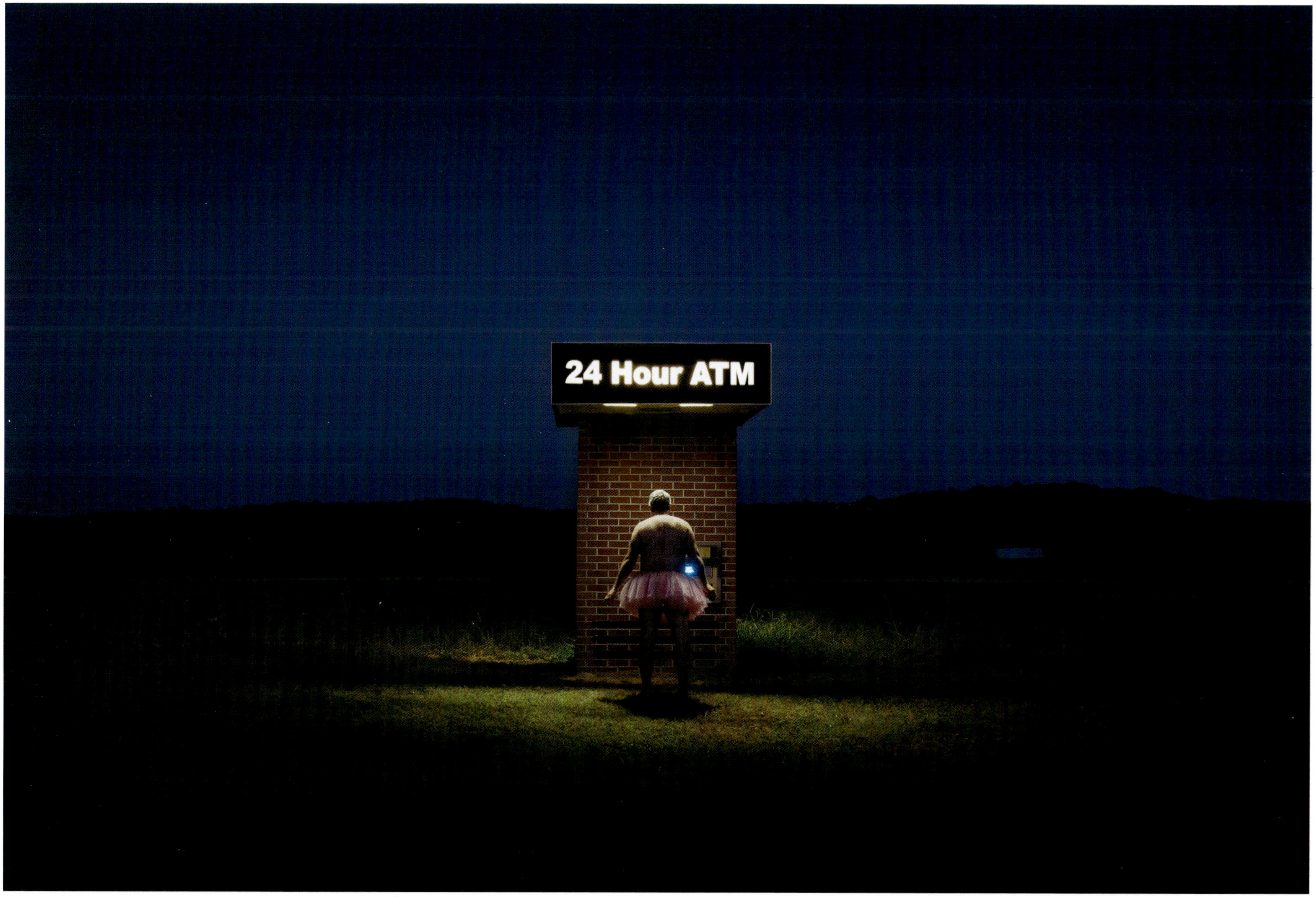
24 Hour ATM

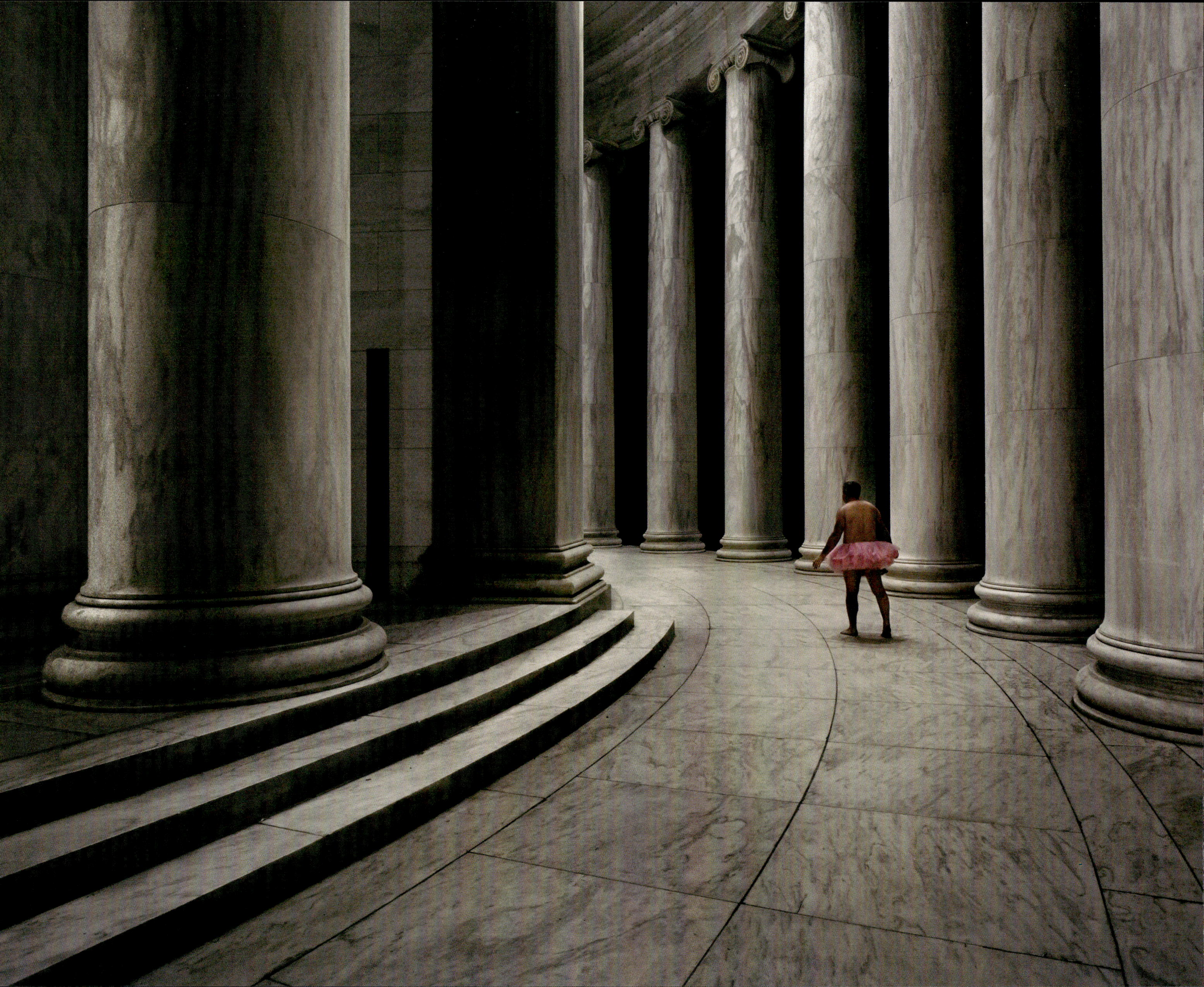

JEFFERSON MEMORIAL WASHINGTON D.C. 2019

Cologne Cathedral

The Tutu Project was invited to be a part of a television commercial for Deutsche Telekom, a major telecommunications company in Germany. The ad, created by Germany-based DDB Advertising, was designed to illustrate the speed and reach of online sharing — a critical key to the international spread of information about our project. RTL, a well-known German TV channel, asked us to meet them at Cologne's historic cathedral for an interview and filming of me making a tutu photo. Meanwhile, our tutu commercial, which was being aired every 30 minutes or so, had exploded on German TV.

I set up my equipment at a point high above the Cologne Cathedral plaza. The second I entered the plaza with my remote, I was surrounded by a very excited crowd who recognized me from the TV ad. About ten minutes into shooting, a single policeman came out of the crowd and didn't appear too thrilled with what I was doing. I just kept saying, "Danke, danke" (German for thank you), but the officer wasn't impressed. I couldn't answer any of his questions, fired at me in German, because "danke" was the only German word I knew.

JUMP DER KÖLNER DOM, COLOGNE, GERMANY 2013

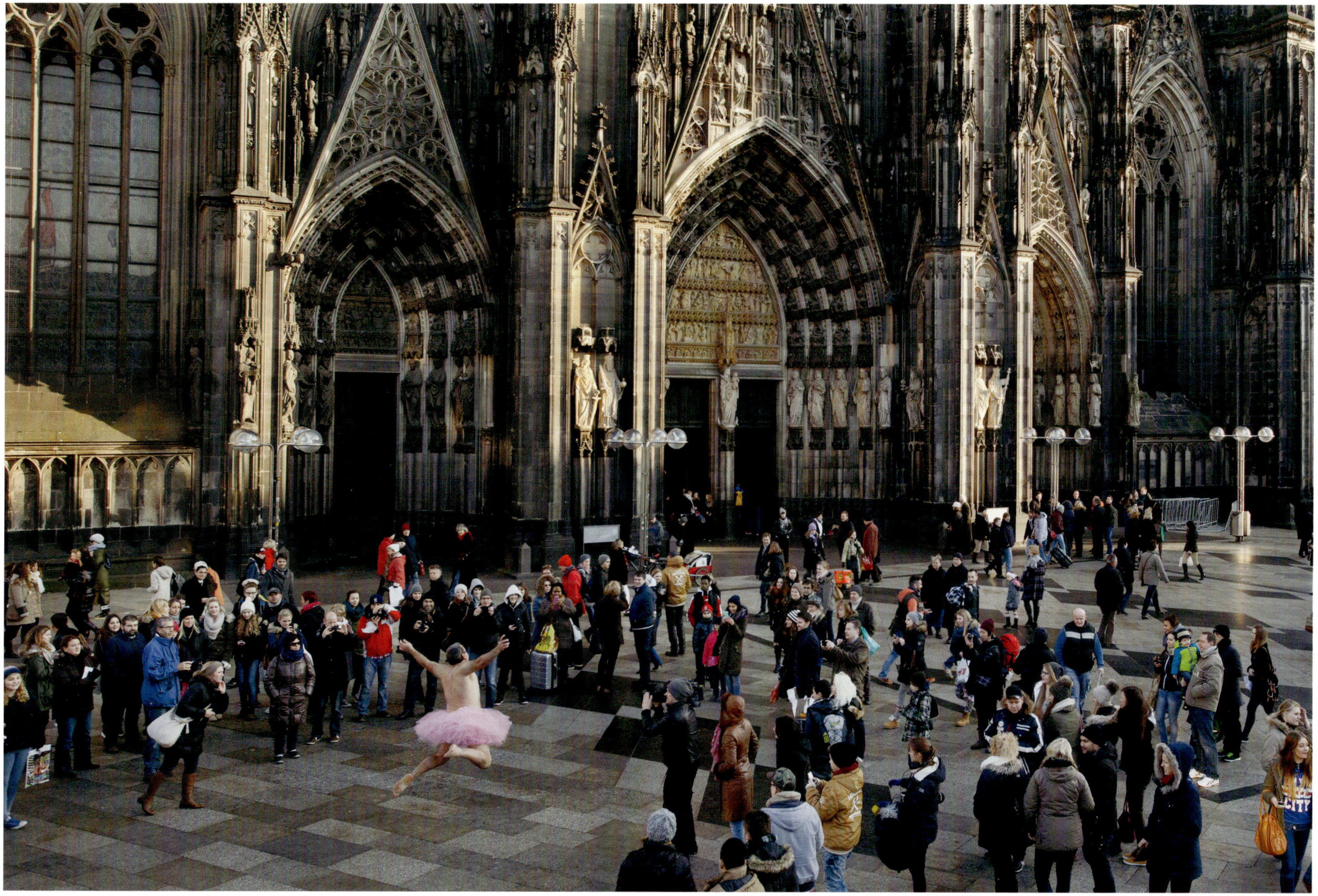

62

First Date

I was near Boca Raton, Florida, visiting one of the Bloomingdale's stores there. During a break, I went to Deerfield Beach and spotted this great pier. I set up my camera under it and started shooting. As usual, people walked by, sort of chuckling to themselves when they saw me bare chested in a pink tutu. A young couple, both no more than 17 or 18, was watching me work. I started to explain what I was doing, showed them some pictures and asked if they would be in the picture.

They were kind of giddy, but cute; I figured they were boyfriend and girlfriend. They agreed. I positioned them standing on the shore looking out at the ocean with their backs to me. I asked if they would hold hands. The girl looks at the boy, then looks at me and giggles. "It's our first date," she informed me. That evening, I got an email from the boy, asking me if I could send him a copy of the photo because it was such a great first date. That really made my day.

WALK ON THE BEACH DEERFIELD, FLORIDA 2014

LAKE MORAINE ALBERTA, CANADA 2017

65

SWING AT TRIPP LAKE CAMP POLAND, MAINE 2014

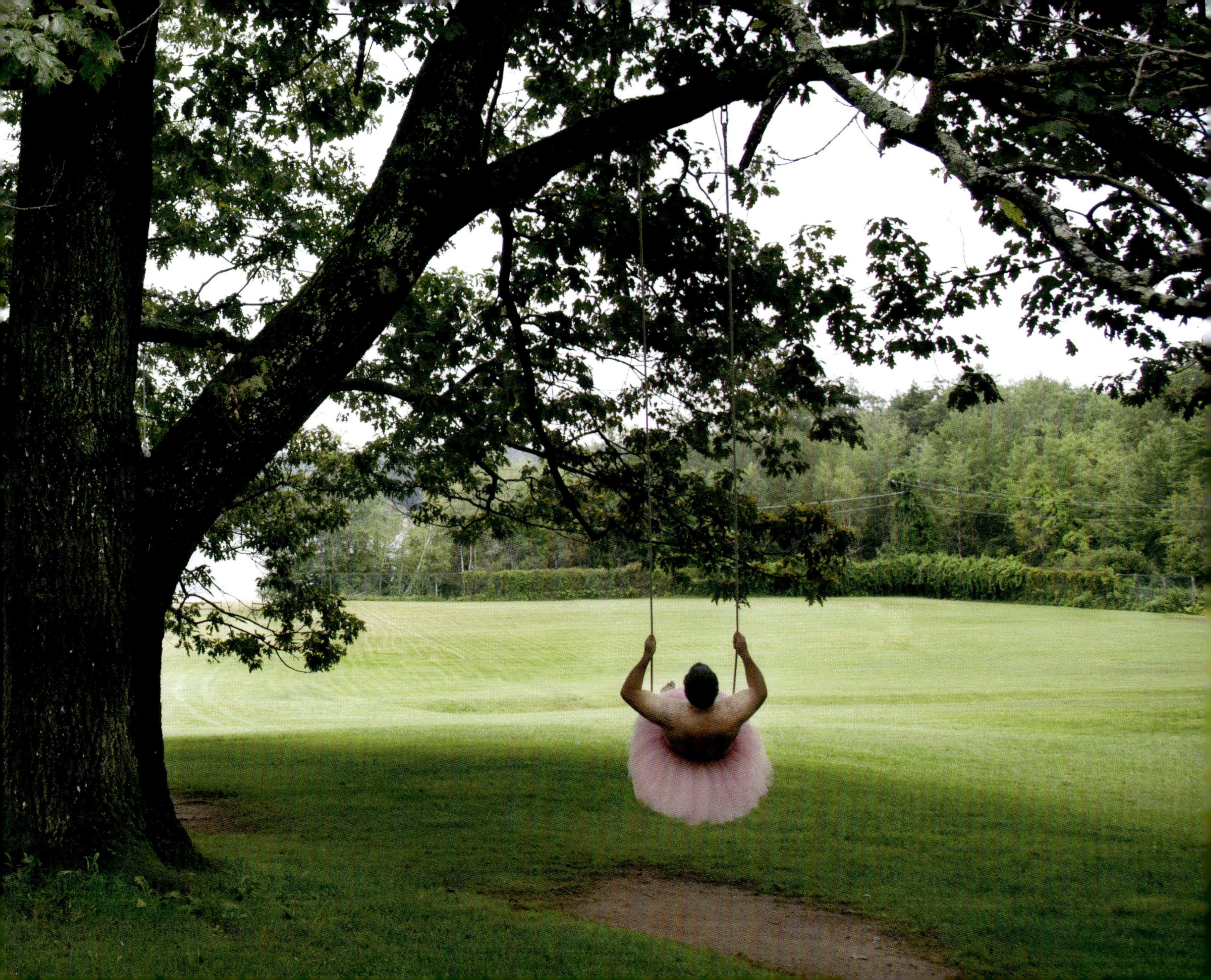

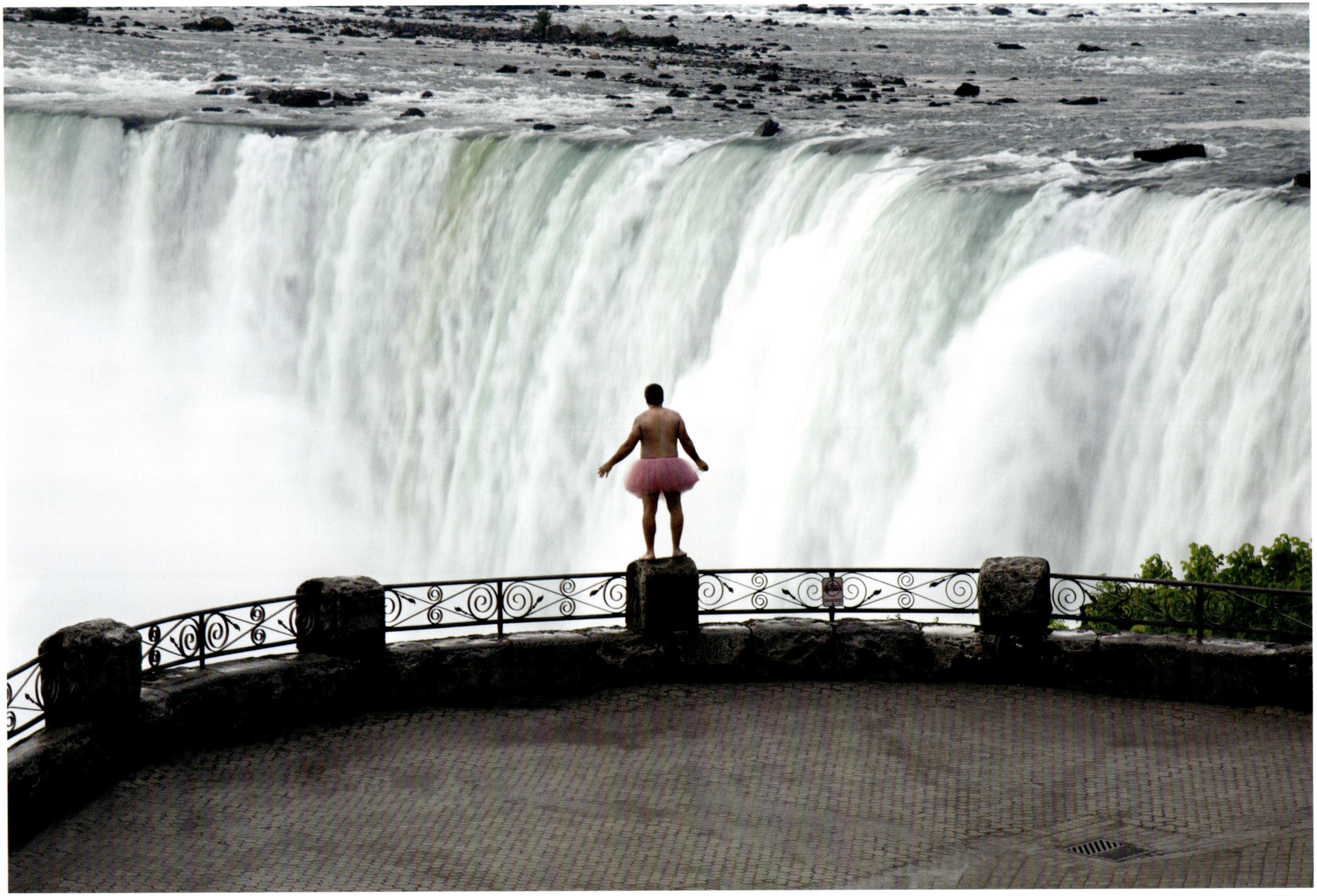

Niagara Falls

Sometimes I just need to get away from everything, so I hop in my car and start driving. I often don't even know where I'm going. When I eventually figure it out, I let Linda know. This time, I ended up driving to Niagara Falls. After I contacted Linda and gave her a heads up on my destination, she sternly told me not to do anything stupid.

But once I got there and saw the location, I knew that there was only one way that the picture was going to be any good. It was 5 am. and there's no one around. I set my camera up, with all my equipment sitting next to it. Then I climb onto a very slippery stone near the edge of the falls that's part of protective fencing — three different times — not really thinking about how dangerous it was (it was a 1,200-foot drop down the cliff to the raging water below). I have no cartilage in my right knee so I'm not always that steady. I finished, got back to my car, and sat there, finally reflecting on what I had just done. I love the shot, but I swear I'll never do that again.

NIAGARA FALLS NIAGARA FALLS, CANADA 2015

UMBRELLAS KALAMATA, GREECE 2015

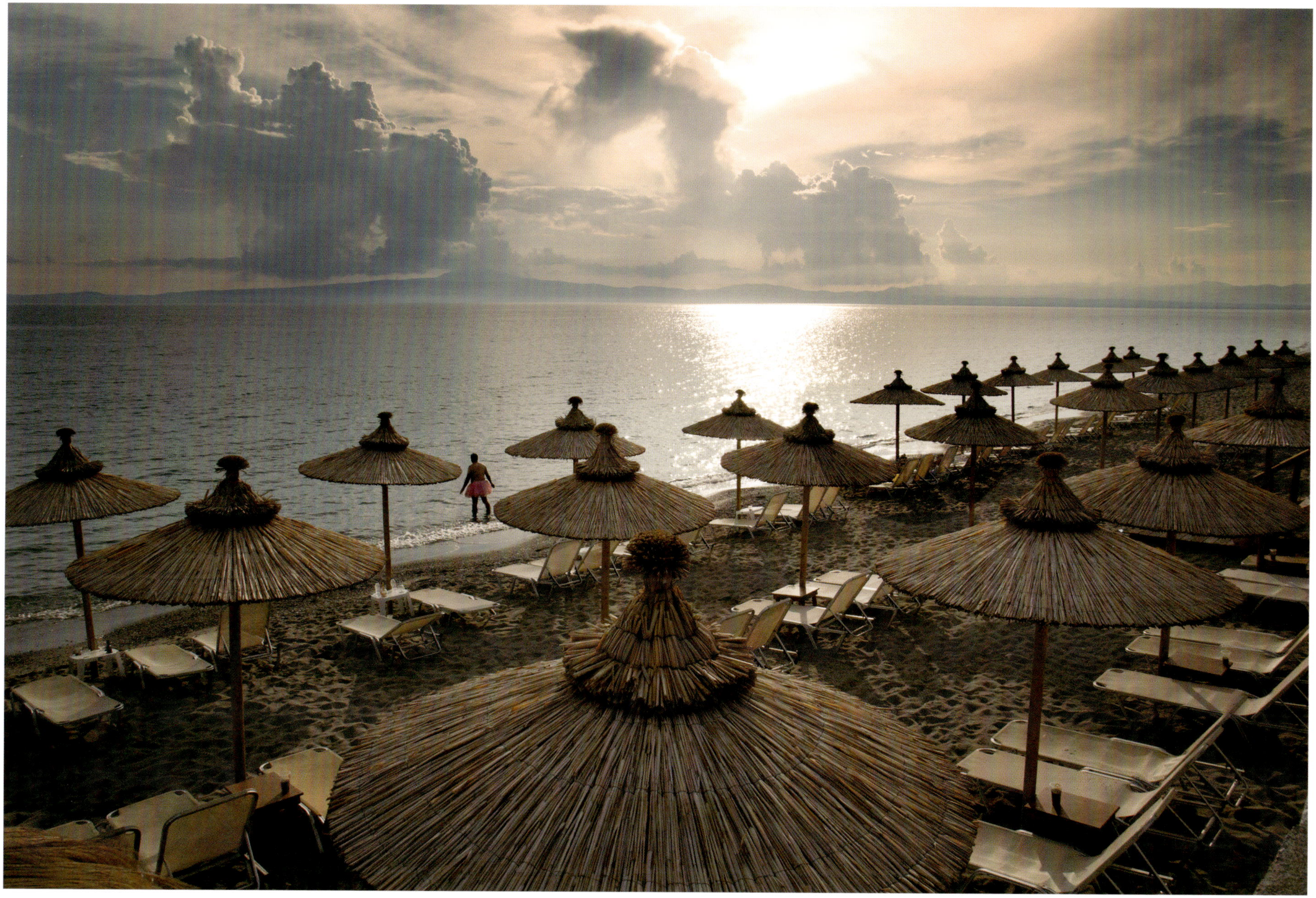

72

Botero

We've been very blessed to have a devoted Tutu Project volunteer, Marcela, now a board member and our business manager, who often works with us on-site. She's originally from a small town in Colombia. In 2015, we flew with her to Medellin and met her family on Christmas Eve. Early the next morning, with the help of her family, we all met at sunrise at Botero Plaza, the town square named after the famous Colombian painter and sculptor. I was immediately attracted to a gigantic bronze statue of a bulbous Botero head that seemed to resemble my own. Now that I think about it, there seems to be a lot of abstract sculptures out there that bear a striking resemblance to me…

BOTERO PLAZA MEDELLIN, COLOMBIA 2015

THREE STICKS PANCAKE BAY, ONTARIO, CANADA 2018

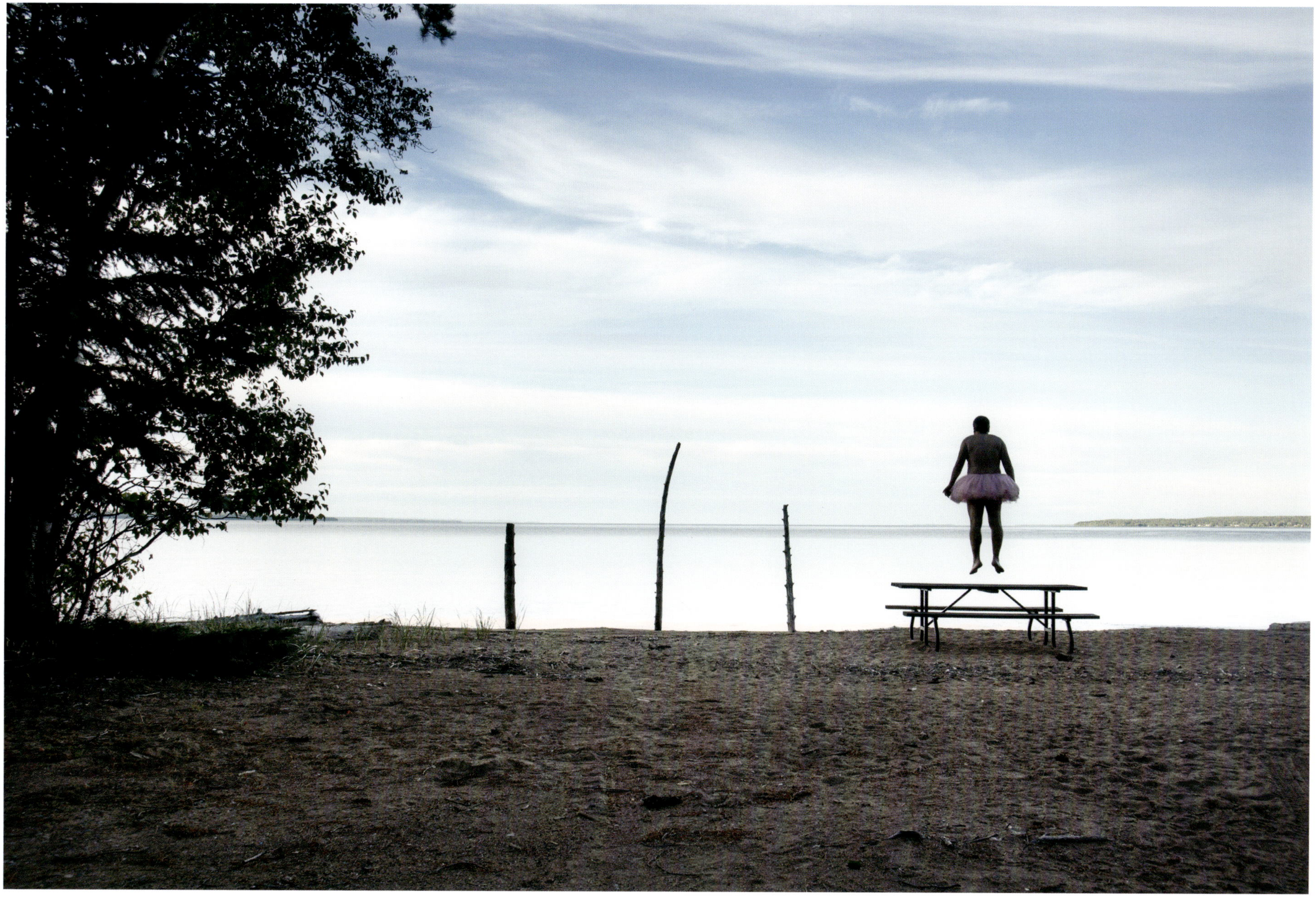

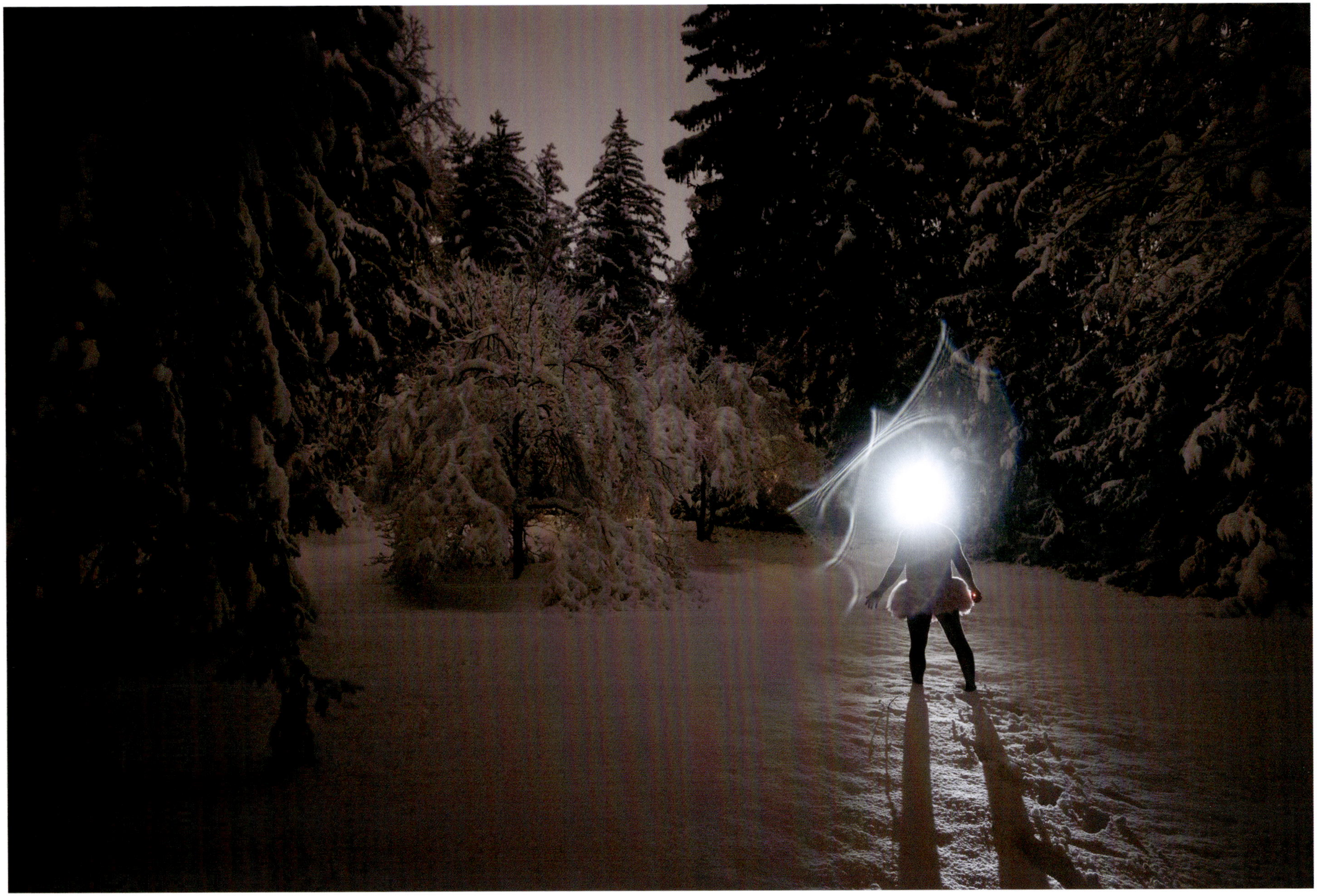

Lens Flare

What do you do when it's 2:30 in the morning, you can't sleep and your front yard is blanketed with ten inches of freshly fallen snow? I decided it was the perfect time to shoot outside — barefoot and in a tutu. Surprisingly, the images I got weren't all that interesting, so I had Linda stand in front of me and point a flashlight at my face. It just so happened that there was water on the camera lens and it perfectly blocked my head out with this strange, magical flare.

LENS FLARE 2:30 AM SADDLE RIVER, NEW JERSEY 2019

Standard Hotel

What you see definitely is not what's happening in this photograph, taken inside one of the rooms at the Standard Hotel at High Line Park. Located four blocks from New York City's Meatpacking District, the hotel overlooks a park created from a former elevated train track.

My old assistant, Chris McPherson, who is now a globally known advertising photographer, was in town and staying at the Standard Hotel. He started assisting me back in Phoenix when he was just 17; I was 27 at that time and Chris became like a son to me. We've maintained that closeness to this day. Plus Linda thinks he's drop-dead gorgeous.

The Standard Hotel at High Line Park has a very interesting history. It was originally designed with no room curtains so that hotel guests could look out over the park. This presented a real problem for people in the park, who could actually see couples in the rooms engaged in, um, intimate relations. The city finally required the hotel to put drapes in the floor-to-ceiling room windows.

I was visiting Chris in his hotel room when we started talking about the Tutu Project. He came up with the idea of closing the drapes and having me pose with my back to the glass window, creating the illusion that I was on the outside of the building. I ordinarily don't collaborate with anyone other than Linda on my tutu shots, but this was my boy Chris and his idea, coupled with perfect lighting, was just too perfect to pass up. Like father, like son. I handed Chris my camera and leaned against the window while he shot me from the park below. By this time, a crowd had gathered to watch me, probably thinking I was about to jump to my doom. This is one of my all-time favorite shots, bar none.

STANDARD HOTEL NEW YORK, NEW YORK 2015

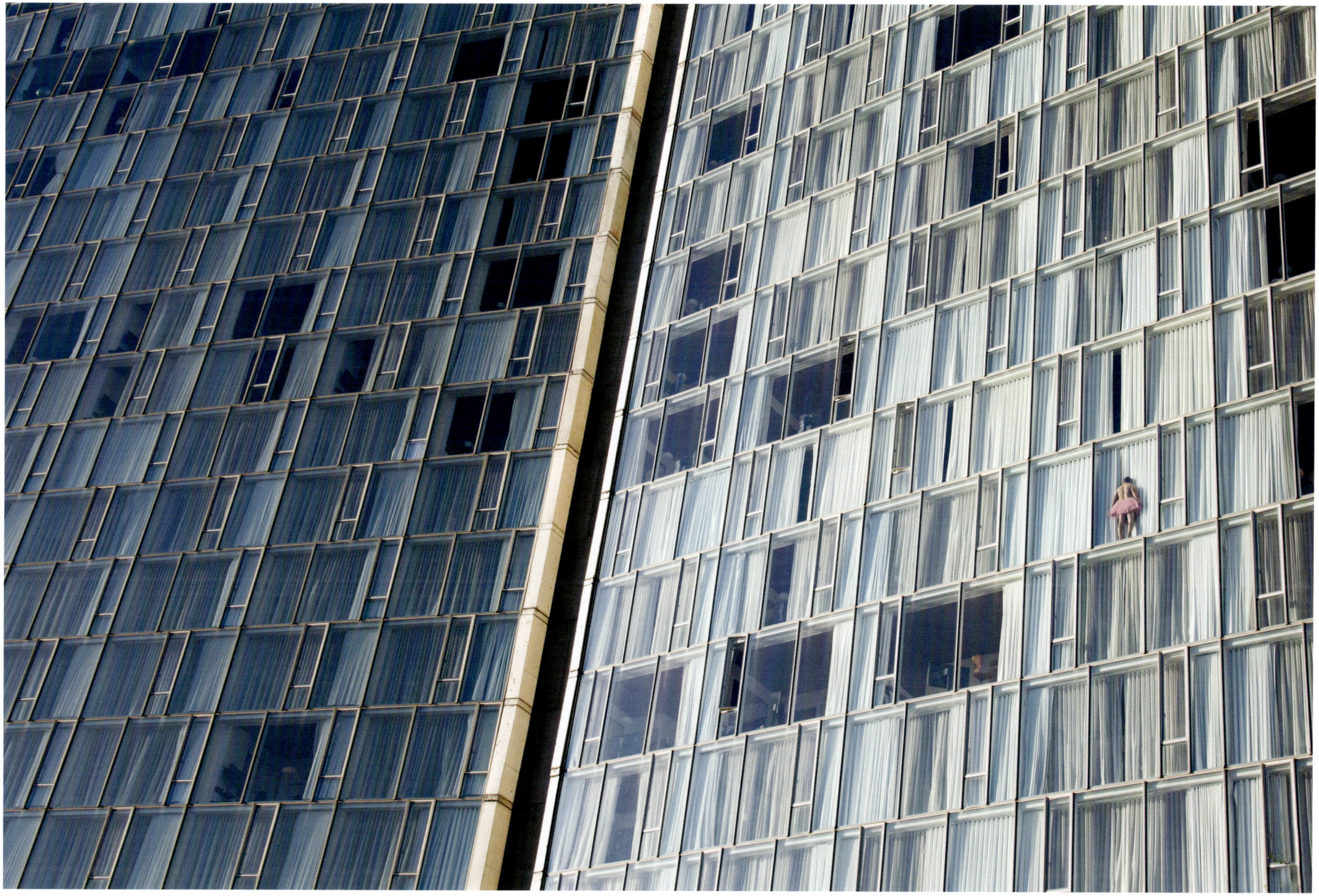

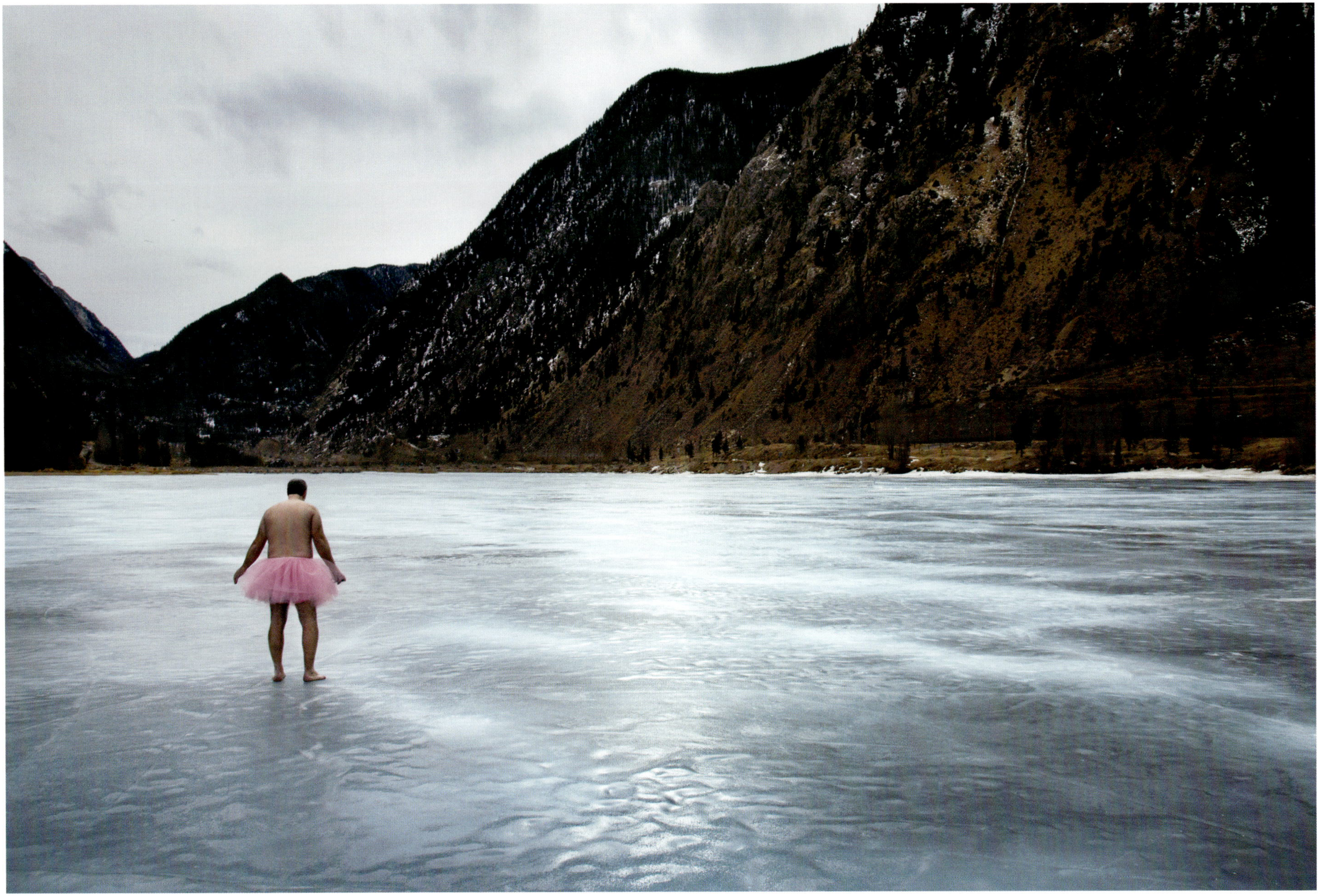

Frozen Lake

My pictures are not always just what you see. When Linda and I were in Denver attending a fundraiser, we visited one of my best friends. He told me about a frozen lake outside of Denver that's used to race jeeps on. We get there, get out of the car, and all I hear is the roar of V8 engines. The lake is such a pristine location, but its serenity is shattered by the piercing sound of revving cars. So here I am, setting up the camera in what is normally this really tranquil place, but all I can hear is the deafening drone of souped up engines spewing exhaust fumes. If you were to turn the camera 180 degrees, you'd be able to see a dozen jeeps driving aimlessly around in a circle. I was amazed I was able to create calm, at least visually, in the middle of chaos.

FROZEN LAKE GEORGETOWN, COLORADO 2013

DEAD TREE STAFFORD SPRINGS, CONNECTICUT 2013

83

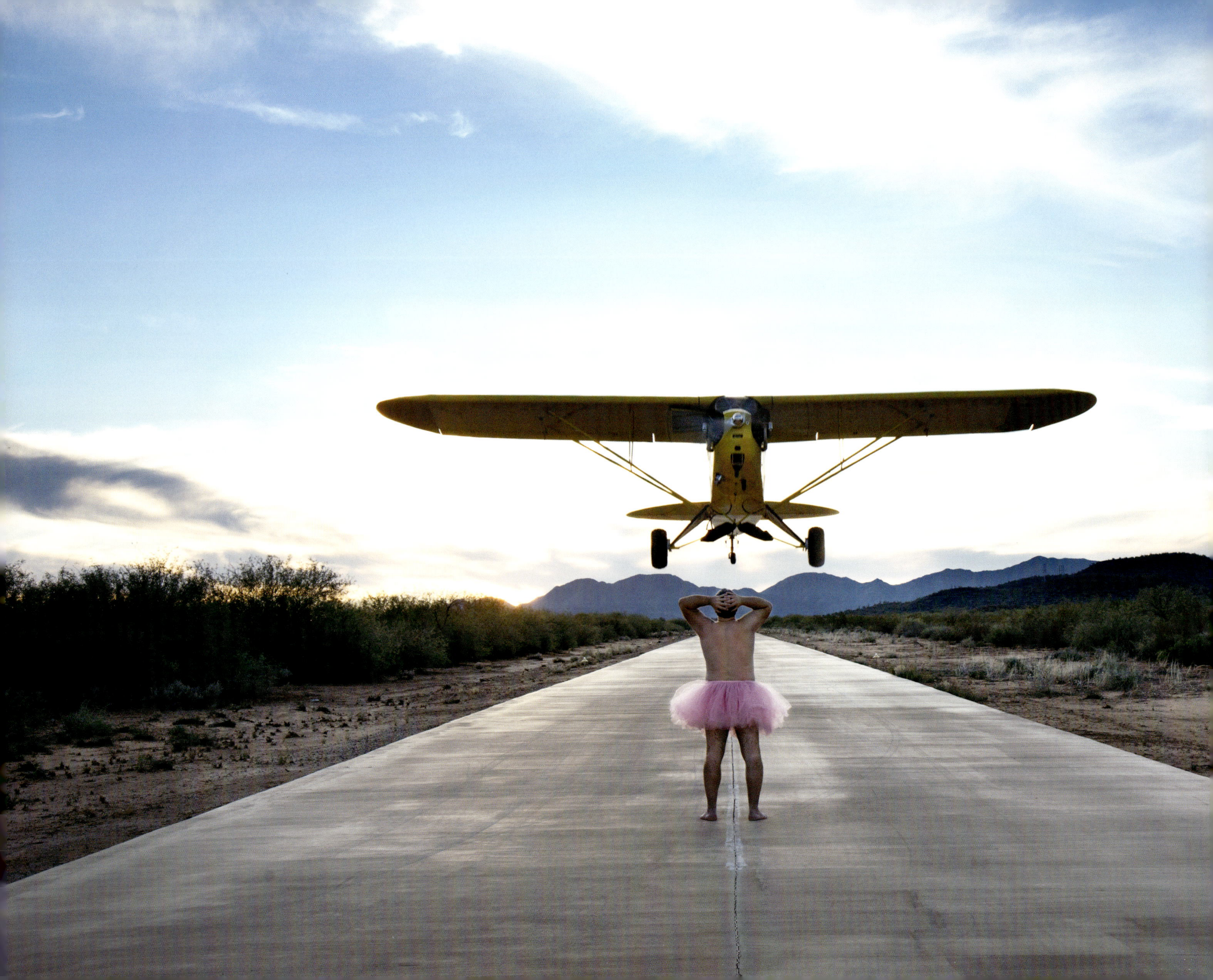

KELLIE'S CUB SECRET LOCATION IN ARIZONA 2013

DEATH VALLEY DEATH VALLEY, CALIFORNIA 2017

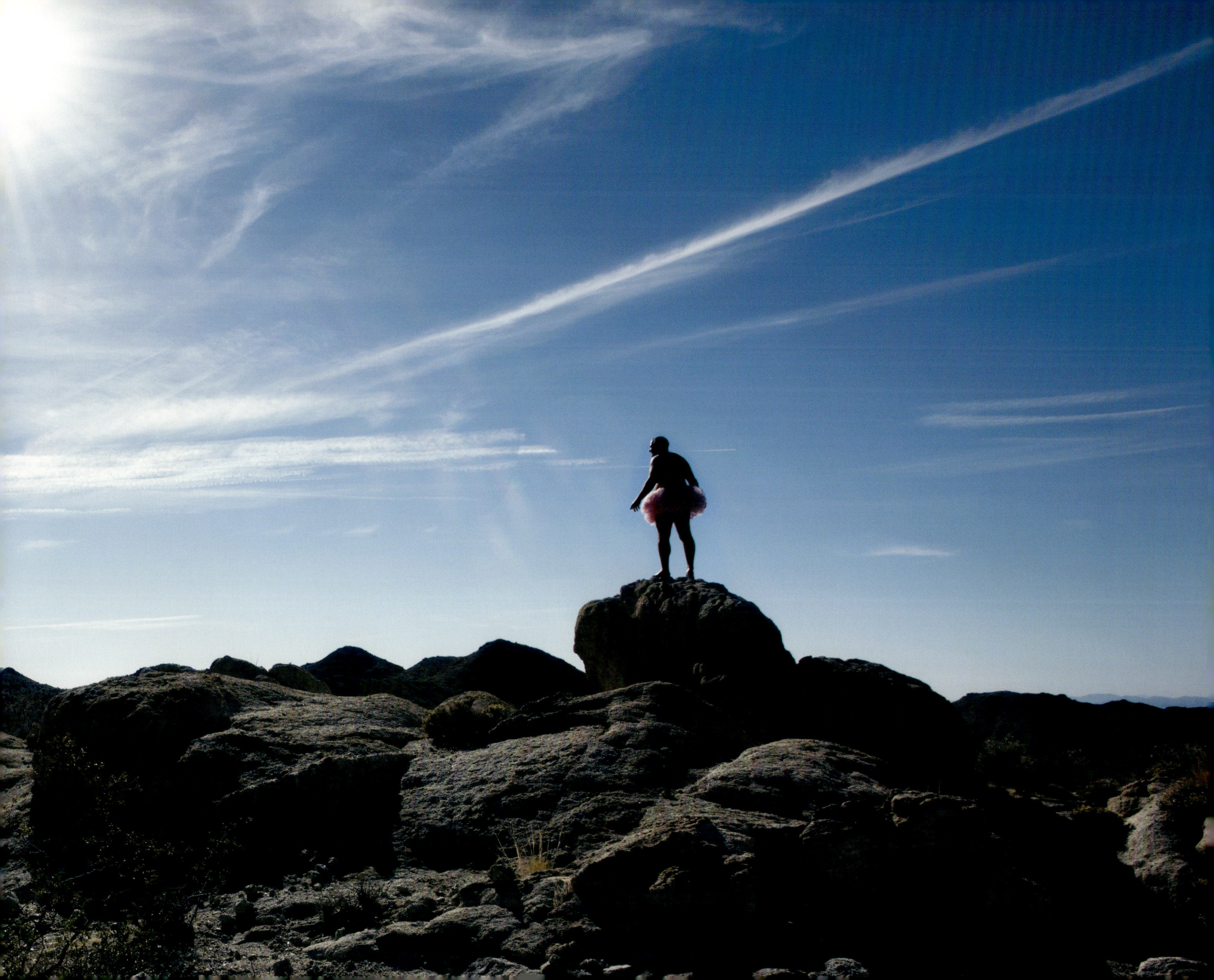

Jet Linx

Seven years ago, I created a really lovely image of me with an airplane flying over my head at sunset on a private runway in Arizona, which was published in *Aviation Digest*. Through my nephew, who is a licensed pilot, Jet Linx — a private jet membership and management company — contacted me. Since then, every year I shoot a tutu image for them featuring one of their planes as a backdrop.

As I was setting up this particular shot, I was thinking how cool it would be to actually stand on one of the plane's wings, but quickly dismissed the idea as undoable. But great minds think alike and my client, Lauren, came up to me, saying, "Bob, you need to stand on the wing." Talk about mental telepathy.

Warning me that I would be standing right next to a generator that supplies power to the plane when on the ground, staff handed me earplugs. Then it hit me. For 35 years, my dad tested auxiliary power units just like the one I was right next to and I couldn't help thinking about him as I did the shot.

We're really lucky to have Jet Linx as a Tutu Project sponsor; they are totally supportive of what we do and really think outside the box, which is a good thing, since I'm outside the box most of the time.

HAWKER 800XP JET LINX AVIATION, DENVER, COLORADO 2017

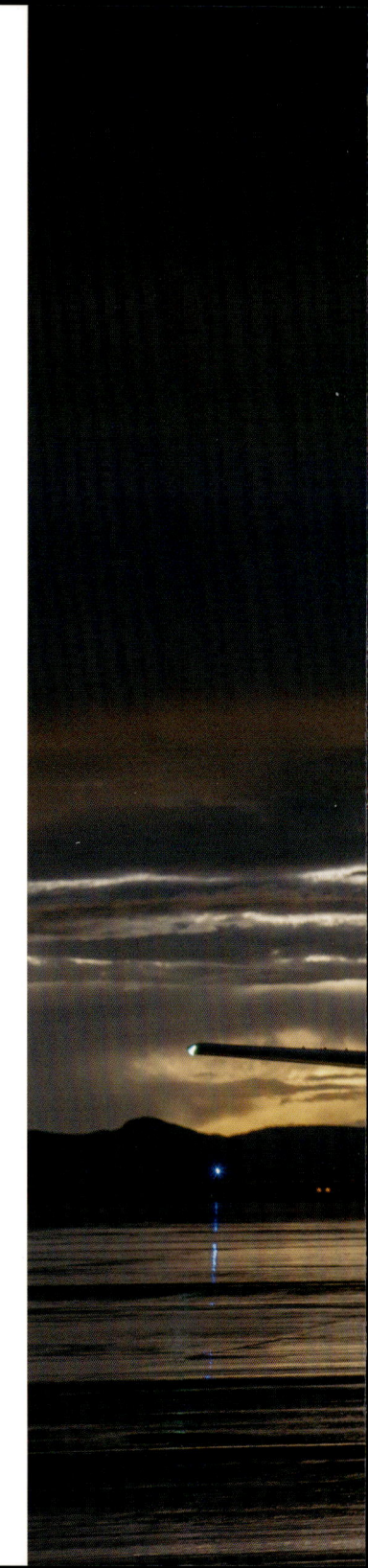

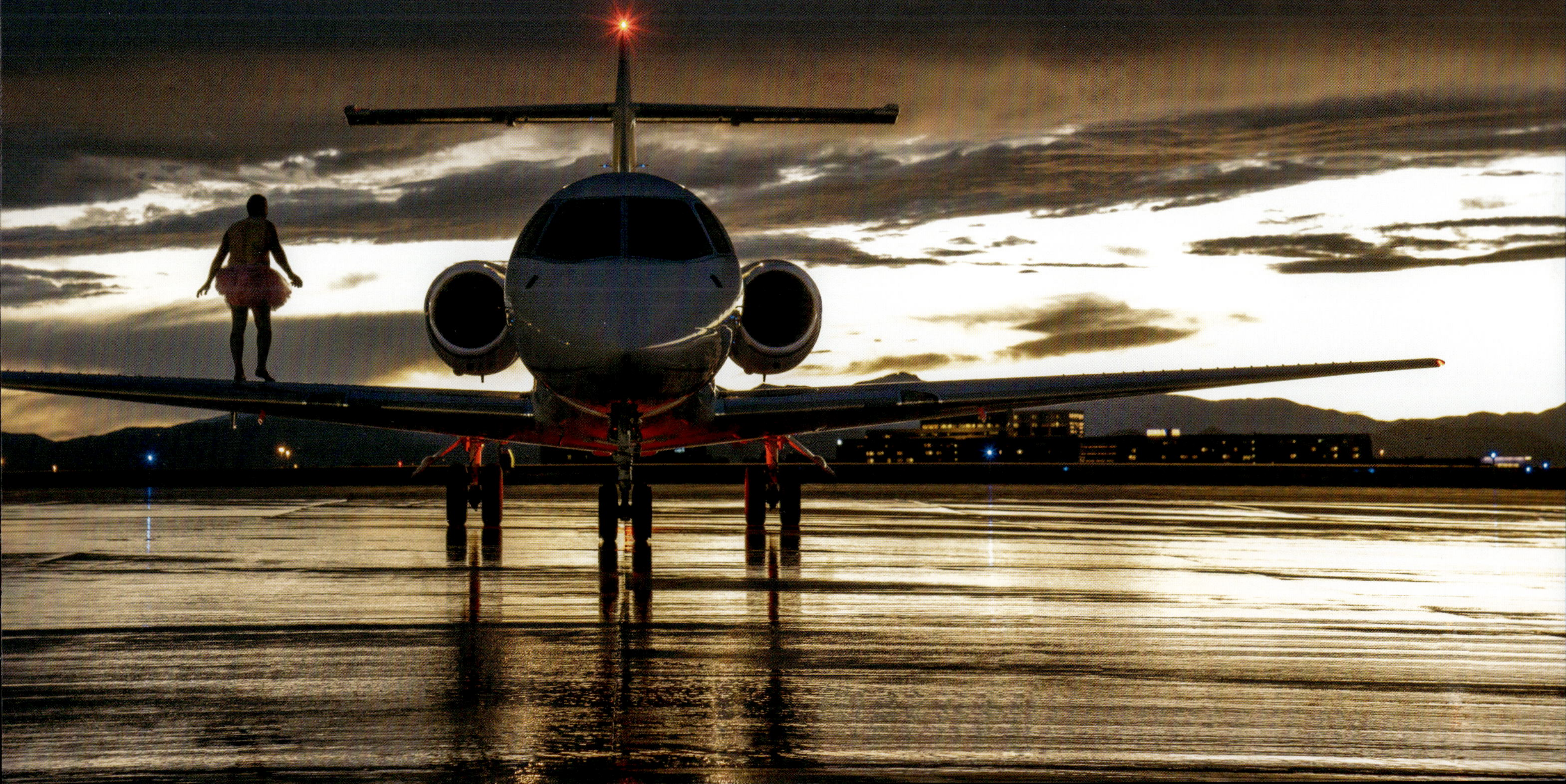

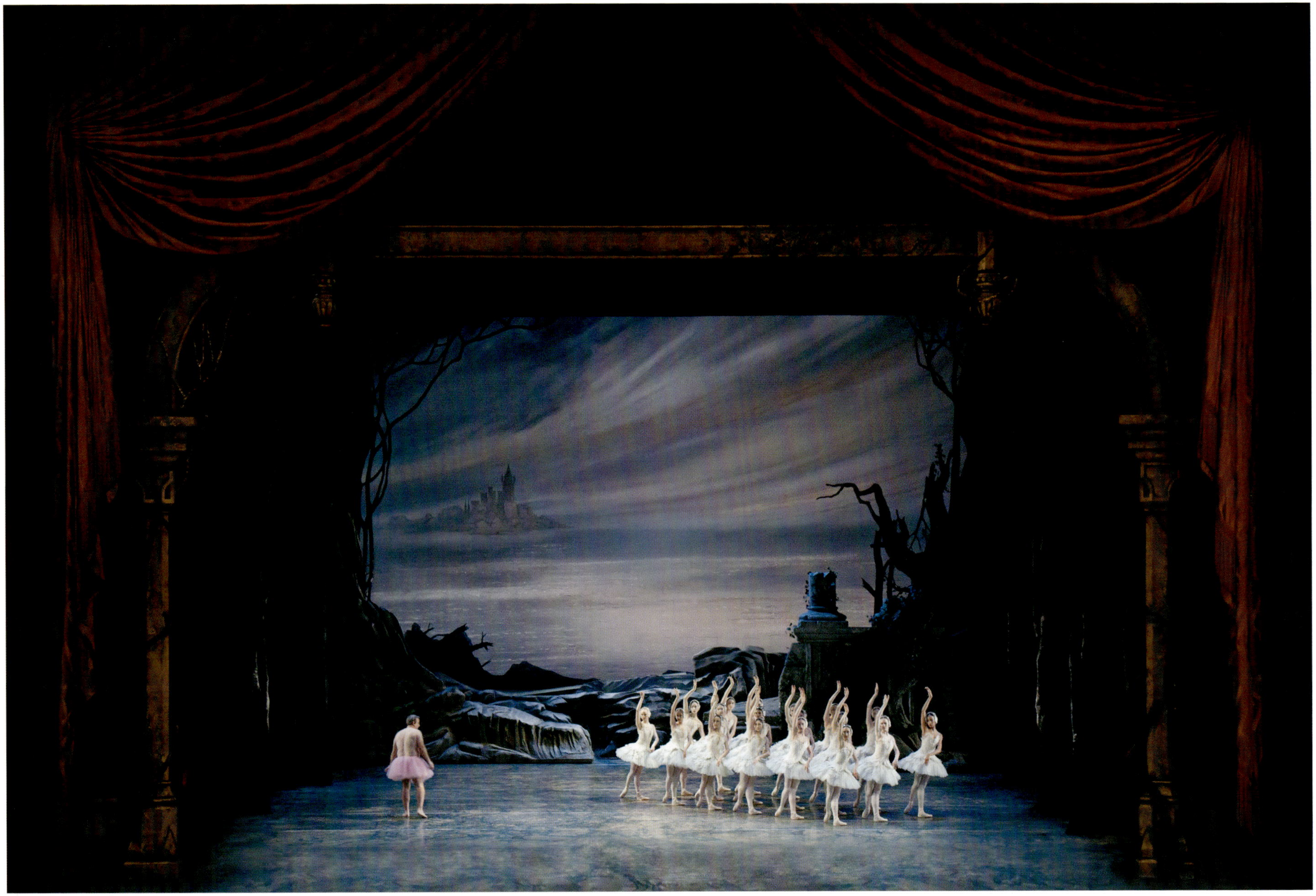

Swan Lake with the American Ballet Theatre

Sometimes when we plan on shooting, we post our location on Facebook. In this case, we were shooting an image in Central Park early on a winter day, maybe around 5:30 am. A man by the name of Dathan joined us to watch. At the end of the session, he asked if I would be interested in shooting with the American Ballet Theater at Lincoln Center. For me, it was a complete no-brainer. Two weeks later we had permission to shoot. I found out from the ABT dancers and the theater's union workers that we were invited to take the image because they believed in what we were doing.

The photo needed to be done at the end of dress rehearsal and we were given only five minutes with the "swans." They had given me a DVD of the performance, and I picked out ten positions to show to the ballet mistress, who helped me choose what would work best with the dancers. I then met with the lighting director; we lit the scene and I set up two cameras in the back of the theater. Here I am, standing shamelessly alone on stage — 40 pounds overweight and dressed only in my floppy pink tutu — a mere 20 feet from 20 stunning young women who have trained their whole lives to be on stage at Lincoln Center. What were the chances?

Once I got out on stage and began to photograph, I heard the ballet mistress announce that I only had three minutes left. I begged her to give me five full minutes of shooting. She asked the girls if they would stay a few extra minutes and they all agreed. I think they agreed because the union rep asked them to because he thought it was a good cause. After we finished the shot, a dancer came up to tell me that her mom had been diagnosed and had been following our project; she started to cry as she told me this. The entire experience was unforgettably moving and personal.

SWAN LAKE WITH THE AMERICAN BALLET THEATRE AT LINCOLN CENTER NEW YORK, NEW YORK 2013

SEAWEED CORONADO ISLAND SAN DIEGO, CALIFORNIA 2016

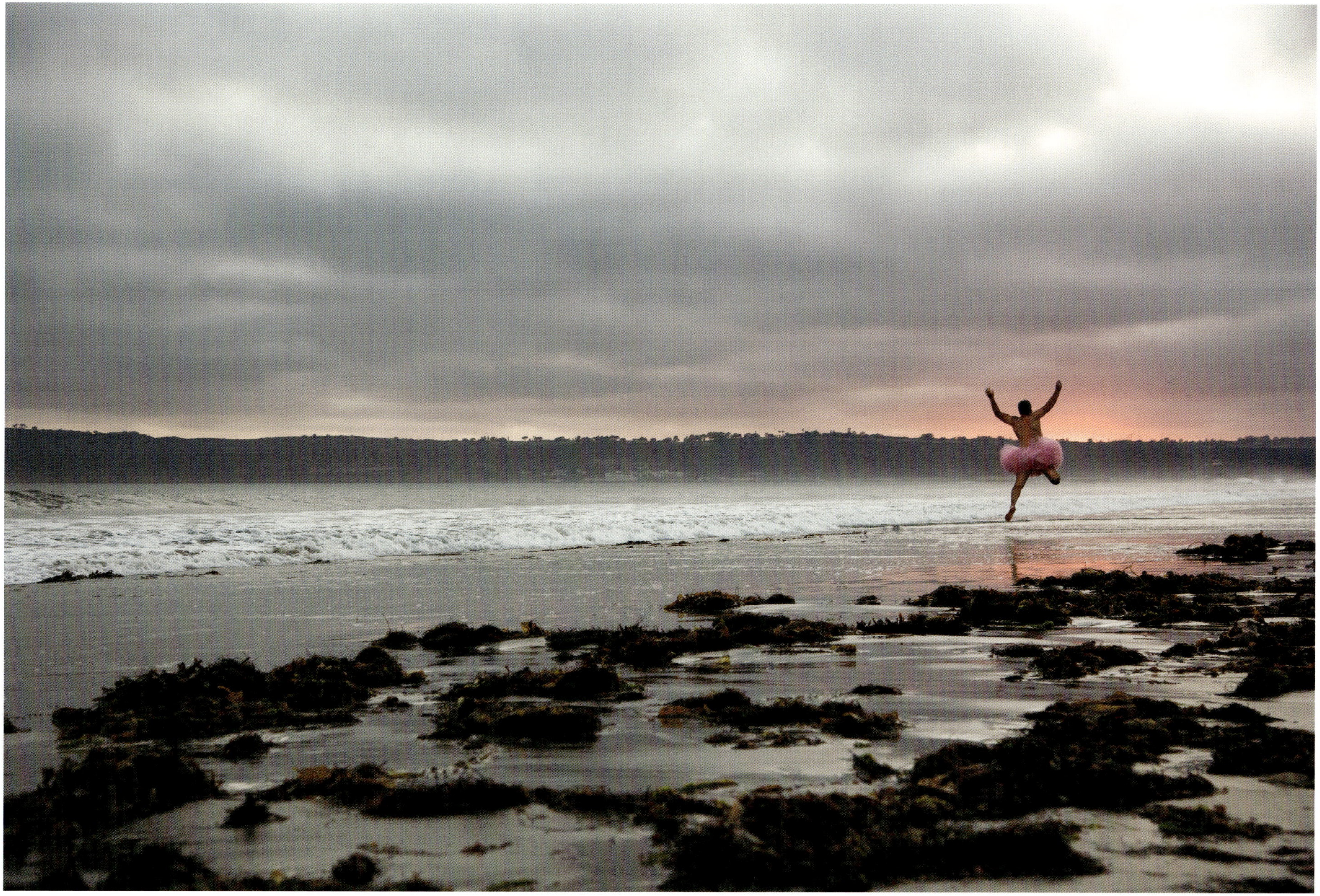

EVENING WALK LONG BEACH ISLAND, NEW JERSEY 2014

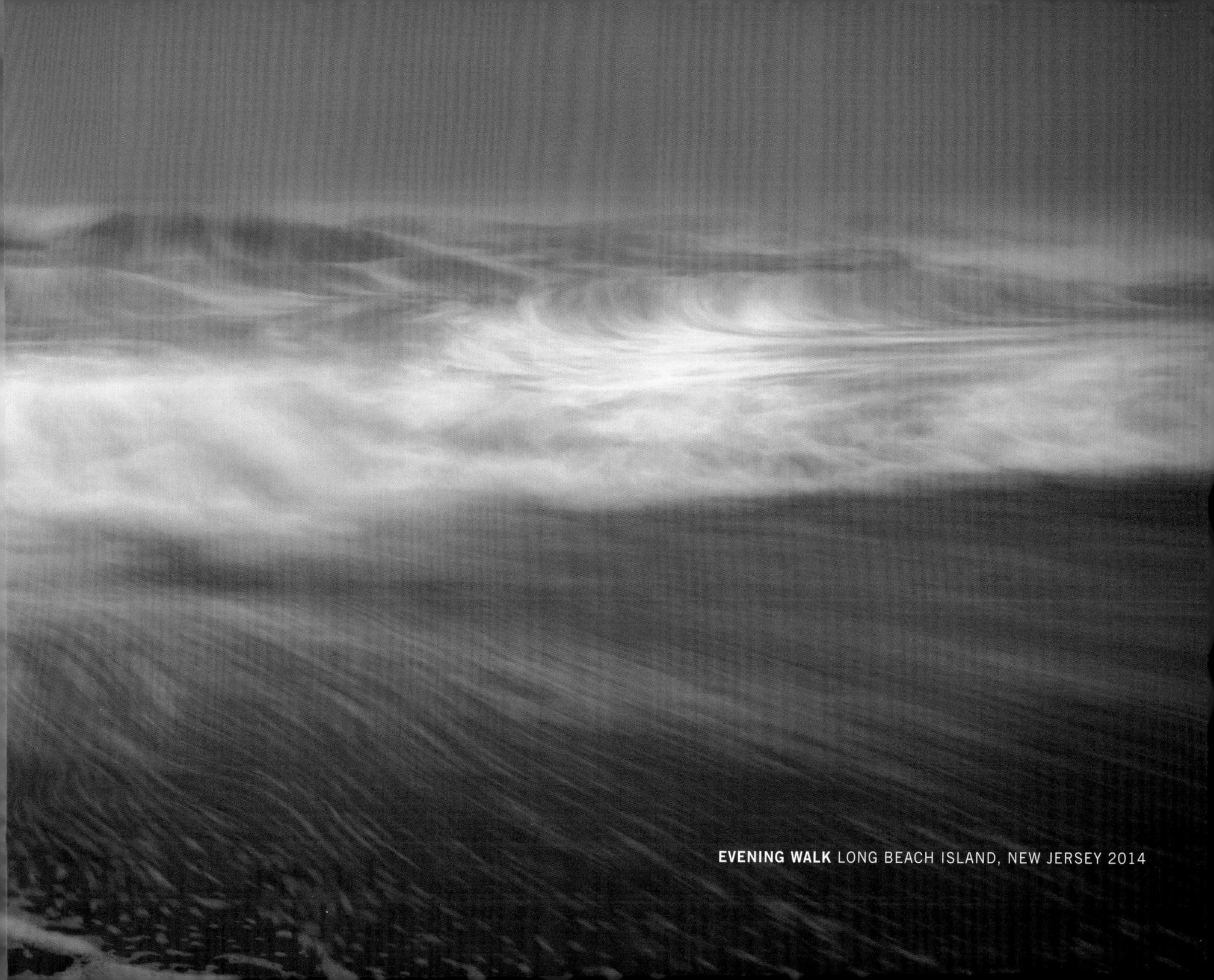

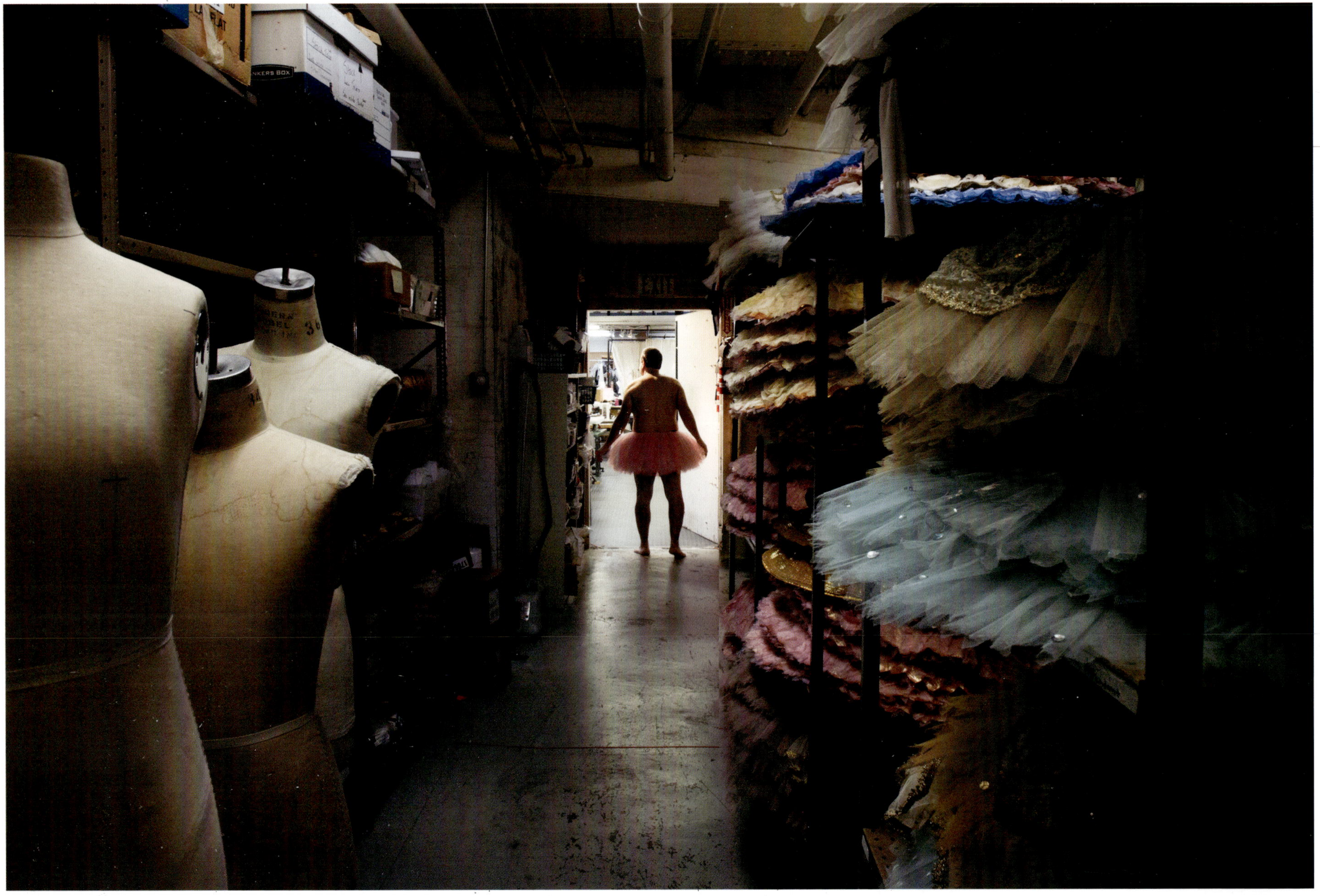